Y0-ABC-412

Start Your Own
TEMPORARY HELP
Agency

Pfeiffer
& COMPANY

Amsterdam • Johannesburg • Oxford
San Diego • Sydney • Toronto

Copyright © 1994 by Business Concepts

Published by
Pfeiffer & Company
8517 Production Avenue
San Diego, CA 92121-2280

Copyright under International, Pan American, and Universal Copyright Conventions. All rights reserved. No part of this book may be reproduced or transmitted in any form or by any means, electronic or mechanical, including photocopying, recording, or by any information storage-and-retrieval system, without written permission from the publisher. Brief passages (not to exceed 1,000 words) may be quoted for reviews.

This publication is designed to provide accurate and authoritative information in regard to the subject matter covered. It is sold with the understanding that the publisher is not engaged in rendering legal, accounting, or other professional service. If legal advice or other expert assistance is required, the services of a competent professional person should be sought. *From a Declaration of Principles jointly adopted by a Committee of the American Bar Association and a Committee of Publishers.*

This book was developed in association with the National Business Library.

Managing Editor: JoAnn Padgett
Editor: Mary Ann Gardner
Production Editor: Katharine Pechtimaldjian
Interior Designer and Page Compositor: Nicola Ruskin
Cover: Tom Lewis, Inc.

Library of Congress Cataloging-in-Publication Data

Start your own temporary help agency
 p. cm.
 Includes index.
 ISBN 0-89384-264-8 (pbk.)
 1. Employment agencies—Management. 2. New business enterprises—
Management. 3. Temporary employment. 4. Entrepreneurship.
I. Pfeiffer & Company.
HD5861.S73 1994
331.12'8'068—dc20 94-4494
 CIP

Printed in the United States of America.

Printing 1 2 3 4 5 6 7 8 9 10

CONTENTS

PREFACE

Start Your Own Temporary Help Agency is the result of many hours of in-depth research into the temporary help industry. Our exclusive team of National Business Library's professional business writers and Pfeiffer & Company's professional editors has brought years of practical experience to this project, and we know that the information provided in this book will set you on the road to success.

Owning your own business can be the most exciting and rewarding venture you will ever experience. We talk to hundreds of small business owners who make comments like, "Doing something I really enjoy makes every new day a pleasure," or "If I had known I could be realizing this kind of income, rather than making my former boss wealthy, I would have started my own business years ago."

It's true! You'll never get rich working for someone else. By capitalizing on your experience, investing time and energy, and studying the proven techniques and business methods provided in this book, you will be well on the way to realizing your goals for success in your own venture. It takes courage to begin. Without a doubt, the first step is the hardest—and you have already taken it!

Introduction: Big Profits Working With People

The temporary help industry offers one of the most exciting opportunities of the upcoming decade. Business analysts say temporary help agencies are among the fastest growing businesses in America...the demand is insatiable–and growing by leaps and bounds. Businesses can contract with a temporary employee at a fraction of what it would cost to hire and train a permanent staff member.

Every day temporary help agencies across the nation place hundreds of thousands of temporary employees in the workplace. Nine out of ten businesses use temps at one time or another. Employers are now incorporating temporary employees into their regular staffing, as well as using them to replace ill or vacationing regular employees, or to work on one-time or seasonal projects.

Employers find the benefits are many. Recruiting, screening, training, and fringe-benefit costs are nonexistent when using temps: Employers avoid paying for vacations, holidays, sick leave, and rest breaks, as well as saving on payroll taxes (FICA, SUI, FUI, worker's compensation, disability insurance) and company-paid benefits (pension, profit sharing, and life, medical, and dental insurance).

The temps also experience many benefits. Some like the variety of employers and workplaces. Others like the freedom to choose their own hours and days or don't want the responsibility of a full-time job. Many are retirees wanting to alleviate boredom or homemakers trying to reenter the job market.

With temporary help agencies providing essential services to both employers and employees, the owner of a good agency should have no shortage of business. Temporary help services, in short, represent a hot entrepreneurial opportunity. They are not costly to set up. You don't need to buy a lot of equipment—just a few office machines. And you only need a small office space. With some salesmanship, hard work, and capital, you can put yourself in the running. Although a competitive industry, it is by no means a limited one. The demand is growing and the market continues to branch out in many directions.

Just several years ago temporary help agencies placed clerical workers almost exclusively. Such workers still comprise the majority of temporary workers, but many agencies have found a huge market for other kinds of temps, including technical and management experts from various specialized fields. Although many of these agencies also place clerical workers, specialized placements take an agency out of direct competition with many of the other agencies.

Especially for the small temporary help agency, offering employees with a specialized skill is one way into an untapped and potentially hot market. Perhaps you will think of an area that is not currently being marketed.

By following the suggestions outlined in this book, you could have your temporary help agency up and running within a few months. Based on predictions for the future of this industry, it could be one of the best steps you've ever taken.

Good luck.

1

THE GROWTH OF SMALL BUSINESS

The 1980s were referred to as America's "entrepreneurial era." In 1986, more than 750,000 new businesses were created in the United States. In 1989, more than a million new ventures were started nationwide–almost half of them by women–and the entrepreneurial era is continuing through the 1990s. The recession of the early 1990s compelled suddenly unemployed people to start their own businesses in order to survive. An upsurge in part-time businesses has also fueled entrepreneurism in the nineties, with people in search of extra income working on profitable ventures during their off-hours.

More and more people are opting to leave their 9-to-5 jobs and stop making someone else rich to focus their energies on building a successful business of their own. For these people, it is no longer enough to spend nearly three-quarters of their lives working in a dead-end job, putting up with petty office politics, unappreciative employers, and long commutes just to bring home headaches and a small paycheck.

You're never too young, too old, too busy, or too poor
to start a business.

Today, the number of individuals who are self-employed is at its highest level ever, and based on your interest in this book, it's quite possible that you'll be joining the ranks of small business owners in the near future. It may be simply a dream right now, but that's how these businesses start.

Starting and operating your own small business is one of the most exciting and satisfying challenges you can undertake. There are no limitations on income potential when you're investing time and energy in your own enterprise. With the practical information provided in this book and dedication to your business goals, your chances for success are excellent.

What Is a Small Business?

The majority of businesses in the United States today are classified as small businesses. The definitions of what constitutes a small business run the gamut from the size of the overall staff (typically under 100) to the amount of assets or sales volume. However, in this book, small business is defined as one that is independently owned and operated.

The major benefit of this type of business is that you have the ability to make decisions quickly and act on them immediately. What typically bogs down big business is the number of people involved in the decision-making process.

Other advantages include the fact that small businesses can provide personalized service to the community or the market they're serving and the owner has the freedom, independence, and control to operate exactly as he or she chooses.

It's important to remember, however, that most major corporations, from Ford Motor Company and McDonald's to Mary Kay Cosmetics, started out as small businesses—as dreams.

It was because of basic business sense and a willingness to learn and adapt as their companies grew that Henry Ford, Ray Kroc, and Mary Kay, and thousands like them, steered their dreams into monumental financial successes.

Whether your goal is to supplement an existing income and to operate a solely owned home-based business from your garage, kitchen table, or spare bedroom, or to start a business that involves raising substantial capital, finding and setting up a commercial

location, and hiring employees, you have the potential to enjoy an independent lifestyle that carries with it a number of rewards. And the rewards are as varied as the people who pursue them.

Entrepreneur
A person who undertakes an independent enterprise; one who has made the decision to go into business for him/herself.

Accepting the Challenge

Remember, these rewards do not come without hard work and the willingness to research and understand all facets of running your business. Many new businesses fail within the first few years.

Reasons given for the early demise of a small business range from lack of organization or management experience to undercapitalization, misunderstanding of the importance of advertising, inexperience in pricing products and services, lack of an overall business plan, improper hiring practices, and failure to meet the competition.

It isn't that someone purposely starts a business without having explored these areas. However, many times a person feels that his or her demonstrated expertise while in the employ of another can easily be transferred into a personal business. This is only partially true.

While it is imperative that you have these particular skills or talents—because selling them is what your ultimate success will be based on—it's equally important to understand how to sell them, to know exactly what your profit margin is, and what steps you need to take to ensure the continued growth of your business.

Sounds easy, right? It really can be. But like anything else worth doing, starting your own business means careful planning. For example, you wouldn't consider taking a month-long vacation without doing some serious planning to ensure that the house was taken care of while you were gone, that you had made reservations

for lodging, tours, and flights, and that you had converted your cash into traveler's checks.

There are so many aspects involved in running a business, it is vital to be prepared for any eventuality. Being prepared means being informed, so that when situations do arise, you know how to deal with them.

Is "Failure" Really Failure?

We have all heard stories about people who started their businesses on a shoestring and who became successful because of their sheer determination to make it work. It does happen, but these people are the exception rather than the rule, and in most cases have had experts standing behind them to give them guidance when problems came up. Others fail and, unfortunately, this often holds potential new business owners back. We hear and read about amazingly high figures related to so-called business failures.

According to a research project conducted by Albert Shapero, professor of the American Free Enterprise System at Ohio State University for many years, no one really knows the true failure rate of new business. The main reason for this is because there is not really a standard definition of failure in this case. He points out that a number of businesses close for a variety of reasons, many of which are not documented.

For example, in some cases the owners reach retirement age and have no one to pass the business along to; others shut down because the owners simply get bored; while still other entrepreneurs file a Chapter 11 bankruptcy, which basically gives them the opportunity to stay in business and continue operating under a court-approved plan, even though they become a statistic on the failure list.

The other extremely important aspect to consider when thinking about the benefits and risks of starting your own business is that having a business fail has never been a deterrent for true entrepreneurs. Many well-known business moguls failed at least once, and often more than once, before striking it rich.

Learning From Experience

In fact, almost anyone who has had a business fail will tell you that the experience was more valuable than anything they could have been taught in a business school and provided them with the knowledge they needed to start another venture successfully. This kind of determination is a valid qualification for self-employment and will pay off handsomely.

When you own your own business, you are responsible for everything. There will be times, such as when your accounts receivable are running sixty days late or the phone company puts the wrong number in your Yellow Pages listing, that returning to the 9-to-5 world will seem like a viable option.

This is where self-discipline, an unwavering belief in your product or service, and the determination to be your own boss will pull you through.

But, again, we can't stress enough the importance of planning, understanding basic business practices, being aware of consumer trends, and taking the time to develop, implement, and update goals to ensure success for your efforts.

Inside the Temporary Help Guide

This book is designed to provide you with the information you will need to start your temporary help agency, to offer techniques to help you with day-to-day operations, and to provide actual case histories of people just like you who had a dream and, through planning and determination, were able to turn that dream into a successful reality.

In addition to focusing on aspects of the temporary help business, we cover such important business matters as

♦ Recognizing the entrepreneurial profile

♦ Taking our exclusive Entrepreneurial Quiz

♦ Finding the right audience for your business through easy marketing techniques

♦ Organizing for efficiency

♦ Recognizing legalities

- ◆ Addressing financial concerns
- ◆ Getting your home office up and running
- ◆ Charting your enterprise's growth

You will find specific how-to information on

- ◆ Advertising and promoting your business
- ◆ Finding capital
- ◆ Saving money on operating expenses
- ◆ Developing a simple bookkeeping system that will show you whether you're facing a financial crisis or realizing a profit.

You're never too young, too old, too busy, or too poor to start a business. Owning your own business means taking advantage of our marvelous system of free enterprise. Earning a substantial living and, even better, realizing a profit for doing something you enjoy is the American dream come true.

The road to financial independence through self-employment is challenging and rewarding.

The opportunities for entrepreneurs have never been better. Armed with a solid product or service to sell, the determination to succeed and, most important, business know-how, there is nothing that can stand in your way.

Notes

Key Points

Personal Thoughts

Additional Research

2

THE ENTREPRENEURIAL PROFILE

Starting a business is one thing, making it work is another. We know that success in self-employment is largely the result of careful planning and an understanding of basic business techniques and formulas.

Start a business based on your expertise in a specific field and focus your involvement in an area that you thoroughly enjoy.

As many successful entrepreneurs claim, making money doing something you love is the best way to ensure a profitable future. It is always easier to address the inevitable business challenges that crop up when you are creating a product or providing a service that gives you a sense of pleasure and personal satisfaction.

Personality is a significant factor in determining what kind of business to get involved in, the way you will eventually set up the legal structure (sole proprietorship, partnership, etc.), and how you will run the business on a day-to-day basis. For example, if you are planning to start a business that is based on your artistic

or creative abilities, it is possible that your personality is not suited to the very important aspect of sales. But without strong selling abilities, there is a likelihood that your goal of distributing, for example, your hand-carved wooden boxes nationally will not come to fruition.

This isn't to say that you should decide against going into business for yourself. It simply indicates it would be in your best interest to join forces with someone who does have strong selling skills, who believes in the product as much as you do, and who will work toward a common goal.

On the other hand, if your personality is geared to working with people, it is a good idea to consider a business that will emphasize this ability, such as developing seminars or workshops based on your area of expertise, providing independent counseling or tutoring, or providing a service such as auto detailing, which depends on your interaction with people on a one-to-one or a group basis for success.

Research shows that in order to address the many and varied situations that arise in business ownership the true entrepreneur should possess the following personality traits.

Ten Important Entrepreneurial Traits

1. Self-awareness
2. Self-motivation
3. Courage
4. Confidence
5. Patience
6. Decisiveness
7. Experience
8. Knowledge
9. Perseverance
10. Drive

1. ***Self-awareness.*** Know who you are, what you're good at, and what you like to do. Start a business that is based on your expertise in a specific field and focus your involvement in an area that you thoroughly enjoy.

2. ***Self-motivation.*** Also known as drive, self-motivation is one of the most important personality traits of successful

entrepreneurs. This is the characteristic that gets you going and keeps you moving when you are in business for yourself. It's what helps you to keep turning out those craft items, upgrading your technical skills, or developing new and improved promotional techniques when business is slow. It's what gives you the tenacity and confidence to call on a potential client even though you've heard "No" three times.

Self-motivation is also what helps you overcome the fears and concerns that inevitably arise when you own your own business. It is the main ingredient that has spurred on people who have achieved success despite drawbacks, such as minimal capital, lack of education, or limited experience.

People with a high degree of self-motivation see the greatest obstacles, such as learning a new aspect of business management, as a new and exciting challenge to overcome. If you've ever undertaken a project without fully understanding the mechanics involved in performing the task or knowing what the outcome would be, you were operating on self-motivation—the conviction that you would be able to learn whatever was needed to accomplish your goal.

And regardless of the outcome of the project, you undoubtedly gained more experience and knowledge than you had before, which only works to increase your sense of motivation to handle new challenges.

3. **Courage.** Courage or the willingness to take risks is a valuable trait when striving for success. A successful person might say something like: "I don't know how I did it; I just made a phone call and asked for the money I needed." It was more than luck that made it possible for this person to raise the needed capital to get a business off the ground; it was the willingness to take a chance and hope for a positive response to the request.

The owner of a small cabinet-refinishing business said, "I always figure that the worst thing that can happen is someone will say no, so it never hurts to try." In the game

of business, you must be willing to take chances. Even if you don't get exactly what you want every time, the odds are good that if you feel strongly about what you need, you will get it. But you have to ask!

4. **Confidence.** The age-old philosophy of positive thinking is a major step in the direction of success. By behaving as if you already are a success at what you do, it follows that you will be, and your customers will believe it, too. A confident attitude is one of the most appealing traits you can exhibit to prospective clients, for it lets them know that they will be getting the best their money can buy.

You have to accept whatever comes, and the important thing is that you meet it with courage and with the best you have to give.

Eleanor Roosevelt

5. **Patience.** When you own your own business, there will be times when you feel like the roof is caving in, especially when your suppliers seem to be taking their own sweet time in fulfilling an important order or when a customer's demands seem to be unrealistic. Although you may be able to hurry the supplier along, you must remember that your customers are always right, since they are the ones who will make or break your business.

If you are aware that patience is not your strong suit, develop a stop-gap exercise to use at times when coping is a definite necessity. Whether you count to ten before saying a word, visualize a pleasant scene, or repeat a secret phrase to yourself when tension is running high, it will be to your advantage.

6. **Decisiveness.** Business has been described as a process of making one fast decision after another. Often, a decision has to be made immediately, on the spur of the

moment. In those instances, you should go with your intuition and trust that you are doing the right thing.

However, if you are the type of person who prefers to analyze your options, weigh all the factors, and make decisions slowly, then that is what you must do. It will keep your confidence intact and ensure that you're taking the right action. Again, careful planning will help you predict many of the decision-making situations that arise in your business. As time goes by and you grow more comfortable in your role as business owner, you will undoubtedly find yourself making quicker decisions.

7. *Experience.* A primary reason some businesses fail within a few years of start-up is lack of business experience. Whether or not your experience is directly related to the business you are planning to start, it is a key component for growth.

If you feel you do not have enough business experience, there are several avenues you can take before starting your own enterprise. Returning to school for specialized courses is one consideration. Most community colleges and adult education facilities offer classes and seminars in business start-up and maintenance, and there are hundreds of home-study or correspondence courses that will, in many cases, give you official certification in your field.

However, your best solution is to take a job in the field you're interested in. By asking questions about all the aspects of the business, you will gain experience, get paid for learning, and find out whether this is really what you want to do before sinking money, time, and energy into the enterprise.

8. *Knowledge.* Experience in your field is invaluable, but it is not enough. You have a better chance of succeeding by knowing as much as possible about such vital factors as business basics, the product or service that you want to sell, the industry you are entering, your competition, and the local, regional, state, and/or national markets. Do your homework.

9. **Perseverance.** One of the adages you will hear time and time again when talking to entrepreneurs is that perseverance is 90 percent of the battle to succeed.

If you are like the majority of new small business owners, the entire staff and support system for your venture is probably *you*. Making a dream come true can be a lonely task, especially when you are just getting started, and ensuring that it works often means little rest or relaxation. You must be willing to persevere during the rough times, to hang in there during the slow periods, and to maintain your belief in your product or service—even when it seems like no one else in the world knows you exist. It has been written that through perseverance the snail reached the ark. So it is with success!

10. **Drive.** You must believe in your goal and be determined to succeed. The successful businessperson does not view obstacles or stumbling blocks as problems, but rather as challenges. To make your business a success, you need to be totally committed and willing to work long hours, especially in the beginning. If you do not have the time or commitment to dedicate to your dream, then you are better off working for someone else.

The Entrepreneurial A to Z Appraisal

Owning a business calls for the ability to handle different situations with confidence. The following self-appraisal quiz has no right or wrong answers. It is designed to help you determine certain personality traits, attitudes, and qualifications that will benefit you in your venture. Upon completion, use the appraisal as a starting point for discussions with friends and family members about your business profile. Acknowledging the strong and weak points will help you prepare for your role as an entrepreneur.

Entrepreneurial Quiz

Use the letter *S* for strong or *N* for needs improvement beside the characteristics listed below. Give yourself sufficient time to analyze each trait.

Achievement: I have a strong desire to be successful in my chosen business venture. _____

Belief: I have faith in myself and the service or product I am specializing in to build my business. _____

Creativity: I am able to address situations in imaginative and innovative ways to reach my goals. _____

Discipline: I am self-motivated and can handle necessary tasks, whether or not I enjoy them. _____

Efficient: I am organized and can arrange my priorities or change my work methods as needed for maximum production. _____

Friendly: I am genuinely interested in people and enjoy my interactions with them on a day-to-day basis. _____

Goal Oriented: I have a tendency to set my sights on preset goals and will work hard toward achieving them. _____

Health Conscious: I am aware of my physical abilities and have the insight to work smart in order to preserve my health. _____

Independent: I am able to work alone, if necessary, and am willing to be responsible for my own actions. _____

Judgment: My conclusions about people or situations are generally accurate. _____

Knowledge: I have solid experience in my field and have spent enough time in a professional business setting to know the ropes. _____

Leadership: I am able to direct people effectively while instilling confidence and loyalty. _____

Maturity: I am willing to work toward long-term goals and do not get upset by the inevitable minor setbacks. _____

Networking: I am willing to develop associations with other entrepreneurs for professional support in my venture. _____

Optimism: I am able to see what is right about a situation and to explore its potential to the fullest. _____

Positive Attitude: I am convinced that I can accomplish anything I set my mind to, and rarely entertain negative thoughts. _____

Questioning: I am not afraid to ask questions to get the information I need to expand my knowledge. _____

Resourceful: I am able to find ways to accomplish just about any task I must do. _____

Sales Ability: I am able to present information about myself and/or my business in a convincing yet honest manner. _____

Tolerance: I am able to handle stressful situations with a positive and realistic attitude. _____

Undaunted Spirit: I am unafraid of the unknown. In fact, I enjoy a challenge and accept the consequences of my actions. _____

Venturesome: I am not afraid of hard work to reach my goals and enjoy finding new, positive ways to handle troublesome situations. _____

Well Balanced: I generally maintain a sense of humor when things don't work out as expected. _____

eXpressive: I am able to express ideas and feelings clearly and logically, both orally and in written form. _____

Youthful Nature: I am capable of tackling work with enthusiasm and a high level of energy.

Zest: I look forward to enjoying my business, the people I will be dealing with, and the resulting fruits of my labor.

Scoring

Although this is merely a tool to provide you with information about your entrepreneurial profile, there are immediate clues to your future as a business owner in the responses you have given.

Add up your number of *S* responses and read the following interpretation that corresponds to the number you scored.

◆ 15+: There is a good possibility that you have been involved in your own business in the past or, at least, have worked in a managerial capacity for someone else. You have the positive personality traits required to be a successful business owner.

◆ 8-14: You are basically a positive and directed person and should not have any problem with improving certain areas to increase your personal business success potential.

◆ 0-7: This is an indication that finding a complementary business partner who can support your goals may be an option worth considering.

Notes

Key Points

Personal Thoughts

Additional Research

3

CHOOSING THE RIGHT BUSINESS

Selecting the type of business to start is one of your primary steps in becoming an entrepreneur. It is not predicated on luck, although we've all heard about someone who just fell into a business opportunity and turned it into a success. For the most part, however, choosing a business is a conscious decision based on personality, abilities, and interests.

You want a business that suits your goals and personal lifestyle so that it will be enjoyable. You must remember that you will be spending a lot of time and energy getting it off the ground, so it is important that you are doing something that you like.

Business Capabilities Application

If you have not yet decided on the type of business you want to own and operate, it is advisable to prepare a Business Capabilities Application (BCA). Similar in nature to a job application, your personal BCA will give you a good idea of skills you have gained through education, jobs, and hobbies, which can be of great importance in helping you find the right opportunity.

Experience is not what happens to a person.
It is what a person does with what has happened to
them in the past.

Anonymous

Your Business Capabilities Application is a personal research tool, so it should be written out after serious consideration and analysis of the categories indicated below. Give yourself plenty of time to work on the BCA. Once you have written your answers, put them aside for a few days and then review them again to see if there is anything crucial you might have left out the first time.

Education

Be sure to include specific courses that have had an impact on career decisions, as well as any courses that might prove useful in the running of your business (art, bookkeeping, management training, etc.) Also, indicate seminars or workshops you have attended that increased your knowledge of specialized areas of business.

Work Experience

Outline the jobs you have held, what your exact responsibilities were, and what you enjoyed most about each job. List any work habits and character traits that proved to be helpful in accomplishing your goals while holding these positions.

Health Background

This is basically necessary only if you have a history of illness or any physical limitation that could affect your choice of a business. For example, if you have chronic back pain, you would not want to own a business that requires heavy lifting or being hunched over a worktable for extended periods of time.

Hobbies

List hobbies you are currently pursuing and those you enjoyed in the past. Turning a hobby into a business is one of the most popular and successful ways of capitalizing on skills.

Volunteer Experience

Include everything from political campaign support to chairing the PTA book drive. Volunteers typically delve into many areas that provide solid experience for running a business, such as telemarketing, working on a budget committee, organizing events, or serving as a spokesperson. Outline your volunteer experiences carefully, indicating details of involvement.

"If there is a faith that can move mountains, it is faith in your own power." Austrian author Marie Ebner Von Eschenbach wrote this phrase back in the mid-nineteenth century and her words are as true today, especially for entrepreneurs, as they were when she first suggested the power of positive thinking.

Other Interests

Use this category to make note of any additional skills and interests not included in the other categories. Those might include such areas as entertaining, a special ability with animals, children or seniors, your touch in the garden, a flair for flower arranging, etc.

Personal Goals

Indicate the five most important personal goals that you would like to accomplish over the next two years. These might include increased self-esteem, learning to complete projects, leaving a boring job, finding a new career, or having the opportunity to express a creative ability. Personal goals also include factors that cross over into business goals, such as earning enough money through self-employment to, say, purchase a new home within five years or to gain experience in the business that enables you to write a book or develop a seminar program.

Business Goals

Thinking in terms of owning your own business, write down at least five goals you would want to achieve, such as independence, financial security for retirement, national recognition, or recognizing a need and filling it.

Writing your skills, experiences, interests, and goals down on paper may provide just the spark needed to help you zero in on the perfect business. Once you have completed the Business Capabilities Application and reviewed it several days later, go back through and review the information with a colored marker in hand. Underline or circle any details that strike you as being something you particularly enjoyed doing.

You should see a pattern starting to emerge, such as an interest in working with people, or perhaps a preference for working outdoors. You are now halfway home to finding a business suited to your personality and lifestyle. It has been proven that people who *enjoy* what they are doing are more successful than those who participate in a business simply because it seems like a good way to make money.

Looking at the Possibilities

The next step is to make a list of all the possible business opportunities that fit in with the information on your BCA. Consider how much time and energy you are willing to put into the business and what your expectations are for the short term, such as securing your position in the local business community, as well as for the long term, i.e., a flexible schedule based on being in the economic position to hire employees.

Say, for example, you like to sleep until noon, enjoy preparing exciting new recipes for friends, and have minimal start-up capital, but you expect to see financial rewards from your business. Your first idea for a business might be to open a restaurant.

However, owning a restaurant generally means getting started at 6 A.M. to prepare for lunch. In addition, the expense of setting up an average family-style restaurant is conservatively estimated to be $50,000... and that is before you start hiring

serving personnel and launching a major advertising campaign to let the local population know that you are now in business.

Taking these factors into account, it would appear that, because of your sleeping habits and low cash resources, restaurant ownership would be out of the question. However, other possibilities to consider would be operating a catering company from your home, developing a specialized food product to manufacture and distribute, or creating a unique meal delivery service in which you prepare the meals and deliver them to working families, home-bound seniors, and other clientele you obtain through a carefully designed marketing program.

Narrowing the Choices

Once you have developed your list of possible businesses, the next step is to rate them in order of priority, according to your personal and business goals. Make a list of the possibilities running down the left side of a sheet of paper and note your goals across the top. Give each business a rating of one to ten as it relates to the goals, then add up the scores. The businesses with the highest scores are the ones you should explore further as having solid potential.

Check your listing of goals once more to insure that you have included everything. If so, you can now start to research the strong contenders in your search for the business choice that best matches your needs and desires.

When conducting your research, ask friends and family members to provide their thoughts on which of the businesses they can see you operating successfully and talk to the owners of similar businesses and ask them to share their experiences. Ask for input from experts, such as your attorney, representatives of SCORE (the Service Corps of Retired Executives) through the nearest Small Business Administration office listed under U.S. Government in the front of your telephone book.

Finally, trust your intuition about the top contenders. Since you are the one who will be living with the business day in and day out, your final selection must be one that satisfies your goals, meets the criteria for growth potential, and features the kind of management and production tasks that you can easily handle.

Notes

Key Points

Personal Thoughts

Additional Research

4

THE TEMPORARY HELP INDUSTRY

O ver the last few years specialized temporary help services have proliferated. Besides domestic workers such as chauffeurs, cooks, maids, and companions, many temps are now being placed in jobs that were never considered temporary before: lawyers, computer consultants, physicians, editors, and former executives.

To the client/employer, a temporary professional offers many advantages. It is even harder for an employer to do without a physician or attorney than to do without a clerical worker. But a permanent position for a professional requires a good salary and benefits.

Technical temps, including computer programmers and engineers, can earn $20 to $50 per hour, while the client incurs no hidden costs like insurance or social security taxes. Often such a temp can be budgeted to the purchasing department as a labor expense, rather than to the department's personnel budget.

Overview of Temporary Help Services

This is a highly competitive business with excellent income potential. The industry is growing dramatically. Success in the business depends on marketing and recruiting skills and a healthy payroll account.

"Shoestring" Start-up Investment: $20,000

Average Start-up Investment: $40,000
(Payroll and advertising)

High Start-up Investment: $100,000
(Full-scale operation)

Break-even Point: Six months to one year

Average Annual Gross Revenues: $150,000
to $300,000

Potential Annual Gross Revenues: $750,000+

The Technical Areas

Cindy and Larry Holloway of WorkForce Systems in Santa Barbara, California, have carved out a strong niche for themselves placing technical temps. Although the Holloways do place clerical temps as well, their specialization gives them an edge over the agencies in town that place only clerical workers.

"When we are dealing with a client, let's say an oil company, that may need a technical worker as well as a secretary, we can

What has happened to the temporary help industry?

It has exploded. Although it has always been a popular alternative for people between jobs, between homes, or in a position where they have limited work time, temporary employment has now become the *preferred* method for thousands of workers in clerical, professional, and technical fields.

take care of all their needs in one stop," explains Cindy. She and her husband both have technical backgrounds; however, Cindy points out, other important qualifications for running the agency are personal. "You have to be a people person," she says, "because you are working with people all day long."

The Greatest Gift

According to Larry, helping people is one of the main rewards of being in the business. "You have a real opportunity to help people. One of the best ways to do something for someone is to get them a job!"

Trisha Paulson started her agency, Select, in a small Midwestern city three and a half years ago with a partner skilled in business. Paulson says a background or aptitude for business is a good thing for one or all partners of a temporary help agency to possess.

Successful temporary help agency owners have a variety of backgrounds. Some, like Paulson, worked in the business for someone else and then decided they wanted to go on their own. Others are former secretaries, housewives, or technical workers. Many are women, some of whom were involved in the human resources industry.

Your Market

Who hires temporary employees? Nine out of ten companies hired temporary help during 1986, for a total national temporary help payroll of $7 billion. The trend in big business is currently to hire temps rather than permanent employees. Overall employment costs are reduced by the cost of benefits. This makes the temporary employment field a solid growth industry, with projections for the next five years expected to be more than one million temporary jobs per day.

People Who Like People

Similar personal qualities are what agency owners most often share. It takes long hours to be successful, so owners need to be hard working. Working with people all day, agency owners should like people and be good in dealing with them.

Paulson stresses dedication. "The problem is, you're not dealing with something you can control, you are dealing with people," she explains. "They sometimes call and say they can't make the job you just assigned them to–they'll let you down. It takes lots of time and dedication. You just have to hang in there. You also have to work long hours. I had a lot of help and encouragement from my family when I started and very little social life."

Paulson made a total commitment to the business and counts herself lucky that her family did, too. "I really had their support, and don't know if I could have made it without them!" she comments. "My mother decorated the office, and my sister was one of my first temps I sent out on jobs!"

The most difficult thing Paulson has found about the business has been collecting from some clients who have a tendency to "string her along." "You really do need to be a good businessperson to make a go of it," she advises. She has, however, found the benefits of the temp service business to be worth the hard work and occasional headaches. "It is very fulfilling," she says. "You are helping both the customer and the temp."

As another agency owner put it, "It is a fun, exciting, and challenging business. Because you are dealing with people, it can also be a crazy and exasperating business. You need to have a sense of humor first off, and then have the capability to enjoy the rewards of the business. And there are many rewards. I am happy every time a good temp comes back, or I hear a client say 'Thank you for sending me this person.'"

Tara Gordon of The Office Manager said that she started her temp service business because she was tired of being a secretary and wanted her own business. "I wanted to work for myself," she explained. "It is a good feeling–a powerful feeling, too–to run your own business. You learn a lot about life!"

Although Gordon said that it is at times extremely difficult, she wouldn't have it any other way. She encountered a mixed reaction from family and friends when she first started, more than six years ago. She found that the people who were dependent on her were the most fearful; while the people who knew her in a business setting gave her a lot of encouragement and support.

One owner of a temporary service agency that specializes in placing domestic workers, such as companions, cooks, maids, and chauffeurs, said that her husband thought buying the agency was a wonderful idea. At first in fact, he was more enthusiastic about it than she was; in the end, however, she was left running it alone.

"He's an engineer," she explained. "I'm a people person. My background is 'active housewife'—I have raised children, been a den mother, a PTA leader—the whole gamut. Now that the children are getting older, this business just seemed right."

The Extra Mile

You have to be willing to go that extra mile for people. One agency owner typed up a résumé for a temp who had good housekeeping skills but couldn't type. Another temp agency owner said, "I would like to have a plaque above my desk that reads, 'You have got to try to please people 101 percent of the time!'"

Learning From the Ground Up

In many ways the temporary help business is an easy one to get into. You don't need any special licenses other than the usual fictitious name and business license to start. Entrepreneurs have myriad opportunities. But, according to the Holloways, they also have problems, which include getting the necessary education about the business.

Temporary help services are different from regular employment agencies, she explained. "The employment agencies act as a broker between workers and companies. If one of the agency's workers is hired, the agency collects a fee from the employer. But in the temporary field, the agency is the employer. The temporary service recruits and hires a staff of temps, then contracts them out to clients.

"In the temporary business, the temps are your employees, not the client company's employees. This makes paying the temp your responsibility. And the temps want to be paid right away. You end up 'floating' the payroll and billing the customer. That is why it takes some capital to start—about $150,000."

What You Need

Getting your business off the ground and running profitably requires

◆ Personnel

◆ Capital to cover payroll until income received

◆ Sales ability

◆ Patience

A Waiting Game

You may end up feeling you are in the money lending business! You pay the temps then wait an average of thirty to sixty days for the client to pay you. If your clients pay up, business runs smoothly. But one problem of this business is that all clients do not always pay as they should. It is not worth it to take them to small claims court, because even if you get a judgment in your favor, it is still up to you to collect.

Cindy learned her lesson the hard way about clients who do not pay. But she is willing to pass on an important tip on how to avoid this problem: Check your clients out well. "It is easy to get excited when your first clients start coming in. But it is the biggest drawback to the business when they don't pay. But it doesn't have to be a problem if you check clients out properly. Find out where they bank! Put together a client data form! Nobody tells you this usually so you usually don't get smart until you get burned."

Lots of Competition

The temp service business can also be cutthroat, with lots of competition and lots of undercutting. "An agency will add a markup to the amount the temp is getting paid per hour for their profit," explains Cindy. "To get the clients, some agencies will undercut their markup. You must have the attitude that you are going to take a positive approach–have a good marketing strategy. The business is not easy. Flailing about does not cut it in this industry."

Another tip from Cindy that will help you stay in business through all the difficulties is: Network. Agencies can help each other in many ways; they can tell you about the clients who are flakes, those who do not pay.

Keeping Your Spirits High

"You need to have a real 'up' personality to succeed in this business," adds Cindy. "You have to constantly attract temps and clients. You can't do this with a 'down' attitude, or if you are lazy."

Another important ability to have for this business is sales ability. You will have to sell yourself to your clients and to your temps. Getting and keeping clients and temps requires solid talents in sales and administration. Recruiting workers, pitching clients, and even preparing a payroll is a big job. It is especially difficult when first starting out. You will need to assemble a group of temps, at least twenty-five to fifty, and get them to work as soon as possible.

The name of this game is service. The more effort you put out the better. The clients' needs must be met. If the client needs someone at the last minute, it's your responsibility to get on the phone and find someone as soon as possible.

You will stand out from the crowd if you make the effort to match the employee to the job with more than a routine review of the worker's basic credentials.

Repeat business, especially from a large company that pays its bills on time, can make your business go and grow! Some client firms need as many as sixty temps per week. If you can supply them with good workers and good service you can hold keep their

business. Your reputation in the business world is all important. As Cindy points out, it takes time to build good clientele, and your good name is everything in this business.

Profit Potential

The temporary help industry can be extremely lucrative, provided, of course, the business is run reasonably well. According to the Holloways, one can hope to bill $10,000 to $20,000 a week, 20 percent of which would be net profit.

"The money leaves your checking account very rapidly if you are successful, because you are paying a lot of temps," explains Cindy. "But once you get going with good clients who pay their bills, you start seeing the profits."

Cindy pointed out that most agencies expect to make a profit "worth talking about" within three to five years. By the second year, the money situation should improve.

A Numbers Game

The key to the temporary help business is volume. Unlike the placement agencies, which could receive a very substantial fee of say $15,000 to place one engineer at $50,000 per year, temporary help agencies just make a markup on the temps' hourly wage.

"The client has a direct bill rate," explains Cindy. "For instance, a bookkeeper makes $10 per hour, then you would add on a percentage to the hourly wage. This percentage includes your cost for workman's compensation insurance, state and federal requirements for employers to pay, and also your profit margin. The actual bill to the customer, in this case, would then be $15 per hour."

Figuring Markup

Experts in the industry say that general sales figures are hard to obtain because rates and wages vary depending on the job skills of the temp, the geographical location, market conditions, and the level of competition within the marketplace. Although the markup on temporary help services nationwide varies, it has been said to

range from 32 percent to 97 percent, depending on the overall market, the ratio of jobs to personnel, and standard local wages.

High operational costs and slow cash flow can bring profit structures down to 3 percent to 4 percent. According to many agency owners, you should have the ability to finance your payroll for at least six months. You will also need to figure in the basic costs of space, advertising, taxes, workman's compensation insurance, bonding, basic liability, and, often, group insurance, vacation, and holiday pay. Administrative costs such as bookkeeping and data entry must also be considered.

In this business, the rewards extend beyond the bottom line of profits and business success. Temporary help agency owners all seem to agree on one thing: The business is personally very rewarding. It is a win-win situation. You are giving clients something they need—a competent worker—and what the worker needs—a job. If you are conscientious in your service, you are playing a key role in the lives of many people.

Notes

Key Points

Personal Thoughts

Additional Research

5

POTENTIAL CLIENTS

When you are in the temporary help business, your clients are all around you. Small businesses, big businesses; every kind of business could use a temp worker at one time or another. Attracting the clients takes sales ability, persistence, and hard work.

Tara Gordon of The Office Manager advises you to expect a negative response from some of the larger companies when you are just starting out.

"If you are prepared to be rejected a few times, it won't bother you, and you will just go on until you get the accounts," she advises. "The problem is these companies want to deal with the established agencies."

Gordon combats this problem by making good use of networking skills. "I get to know people in town," she explains. "You have got to join groups and organizations—get out there—let people know you exist, and talk about what you do!"

Many temp service owners who are just starting out begin developing their contact with client firms by making outside sales calls and by becoming involved with local business organizations such as the chamber of commerce or small business owners' networking groups. Advertisements in local and regional business publications, as well as the Yellow Pages, help make clients and potential employees aware of your services.

When a company needs a temp, the purchasing manager or the department manager simply places a call to a temporary help agency. They often call two or three different services. They shop around to get the best deal. You have to do your best to see that you are the one they pick.

Landing a contract with one of your area's larger companies can be important to your long-term success and help attract good temps. The large companies can afford to pay top money and to use temps in large number.

Guidelines for Clients

Let companies know what you have to offer. If you offer top service, they may decide to go with you, especially if they are unhappy with the agency they are currently using. In a recent publication of the National Association of Temporary Services, business owners are given five tips for evaluating temporary services. These are what companies are told to look for when considering your services:

1. Since you are paying for a temp who is backed by a professional team, ask to see customer references about the firm's management and staff qualifications.

2. Learn how the firm recruits and retains qualified, reliable personnel who are available when you need them. Check your local newspaper's classified section, or ask to see their recruitment ads.

3. Are employees thoroughly screened, tested, interviewed, and acquainted with the position they are filling?

4. Does the firm determine the special needs of your company and carefully match that information with fully developed employee work files? If not, you may end up paying for a temporary secretary when the job requires a less costly receptionist. Or you may lose time if a receptionist is assigned to your company when a first-rate secretary is needed.

5. If the firm is a member of the National Association of Temporary Services, you can assume it has pledged to abide by codes of good practice.

Use these guidelines developed for people considering using temporary services as your own checklist in running the business. It will help you keep your standards high and ensure clients that they are going to get top quality service and the best temps available.

The Broad View of the Market

The temporary employment industry's growth has opened up a myriad of opportunities for the smart entrepreneur. It is a $10 billion industry nationwide, and many smart businesspeople are seeing the potential and cashing in on the boom. Many, also, are seeing a new wrinkle—a new specialization—and are opening up yet untapped and unexploited markets.

At the same time, the industry's growth has fostered stiff competition among agencies. Franchisers and independents alike are playing the field. It can be very competitive out there. Small firms must compete with national firms with franchise offices. Often those firms are doing business with other national firms having branches nationwide, because they only have to negotiate the contract once.

Getting the Upper Hand

Yet many a small temporary help business is surviving and thriving. Many independently owned small temp agencies are finding their business very lucrative and satisfying.

In particular, surveys show that small agencies owned by women have some advantages over a large franchise operation. They are getting government contracts because firms working on government contracts are sensitive to meeting their quotas for doing business with minority owned firms.

In addition, small firms have an advantage over large firms in the specialized market. They stand out, when they specialize in an area in which they do best. They can attract people who would never sign up with a big name regular temp service.

Also, there is constant and insatiable need for temporary services. There is a lot of business. And companies are constantly shopping around. Clients are looking not just for a big name, but good service, good prices, and good temps.

One of the hottest new ideas in temporary employment is placement of professionals, including doctors, lawyers, accountants, and architects who fill in for periods from a few weeks to a few years. In this case, the profits are higher because you are working with high ticket recruits and clients willing to pay handsomely for their specialized training.

Finding Temp Workers

The ranks of available temporary workers are largest during the summer, when students are job hunting, and in the fall when women with school-age children reenter the work force. The business, like any other, has its peak times and its lean times.

Smart agency owners keep an eye on their overhead by employing just the right amount of full-time staffers to make the business grow and make money, but not to eat up profits. A good sized agency may only need ten full time staffers to handle administration, sales, and recruitment. Many owners also flnd it good practice to have computers maintain client lists, billing, and payroll, and to get good accounting help. This can be critical in the early stages of the business, since the temps must be paid weekly even though clients are billed monthly. The process can be complex and draining to a new business.

And despite the temporary service industry's boom nationwide, and even if profits are soaring, a smart agency owner continues to keep up high standards of service and aggressive sales. Your agency's good name is vital to your continued success.

Ground Floor Marketing

Make a list of everyone you know. Even if the names on your list seem unrealistic as far as potential clients go, keep in mind that they may know someone else who might have a need for your services at some future time. Your list will help you preplan your business approach, develop your sales skills in promoting the business, and recruit new clients.

Start your list by including the names of the following people. You will probably think of other contacts not listed here, but this will give you a strong starting point.

♦ Relatives who live in the area

♦ Acquaintances from social groups or hobbies

♦ People from the market, the barber, beautician, and local retailers where you do business regularly

♦ Your doctor, lawyer, banker, plumber, gardener, and other service providers

♦ People you know in professional offices, including real estate brokers, insurance agents, and executives

♦ The mail carrier, landlord, and your children's teachers

♦ Friends from work, school, church, etc.

Talk to everyone on your list to find out whether they have a need for your services, or if they can give you the name of someone they know who might be a potential client. Give out business cards and brochures and ask everyone to pass them along—people love to help and will probably be happy to lend a hand in getting your business off the ground.

Potential Customers

Friends and Relatives

Acquaintances and Service Providers

Business Contacts

6

A MARKETING OVERVIEW

Now that you have selected the kind of business you want to own, it is important to explore the need for it. A process known as *marketing research* will provide you with the information you need to develop your business, plan methods of distribution or promotion, and set prices that are tailored to the audience you hope to attract.

In addition, your marketing research will provide you with information that will help when you make decisions about a location, hours of operation, the specific types of services and/or products to sell, and how to gear your advertising.

Identifying Your Market

The process of identifying your audience may seem to be an extremely complex process; however, you can develop a perfectly workable and valuable marketing report by using the following guidelines and adapting them to your particular situation. Basically, there are five factors used to target the market.

Five Factors Used to Target Your Market

1. Population
2. Income
3. Competition
4. Product or service market match
5. Desire

1. ***Population.*** The number of households in the region you are considering for your business is crucial, as you must have a sufficient population base to produce the sales you need to generate a profit. Equally important is the circulation and age range of readers of the publications where you will be placing your advertising. If, for example, you are planning to sell products for infants, a publication whose readership is largely of retirement age would be inappropriate. It would, however, work in your favor if you were promoting health products or gift items. If you are selling a computer-based service, you might consider computer trade publications.

2. ***Income.*** Your potential customers must have the income to purchase goods and services. Consumers in the thirty-five to sixty-five age group generally have considerable income to spend on household items, personal grooming, and sporting goods. This is not to discount the over-sixty-five age group, a large and growing segment of the nation's population which, depending on the region, has adequate discretionary income (money after taxes and necessities) to spend, or the eighteen to thirty-five age group, which is a desirable market for clothing, personal, and recreational items.

3. ***Competition.*** Competition shouldn't be a negative factor. Rather, it should spur you on to stretch your creativity by creating something brand new or creating a similar

product or service that is superior to those being offered by the competition–through quality, selection, or price.

4. ***Product or service market match.*** Basically, this means that you must be able to attract those consumers whom you have the resources to serve. For example, if your idea of the perfect business involves national distribution of your patented weight-training equipment, you must reach an audience that is receptive and interested in bodybuilding through a carefully designed advertising campaign, and have the financing available to supply and ship the product.

5. ***Desire.*** Your objective is to match your product or service to the needs and desires of a particular group of consumers who will be responsive. It is often difficult to figure out exactly what your target market wants. However, through observation of what the competition is doing, it should be possible to recognize a need.

Market Research Techniques

Large corporations often have in-house marketing staffs who conduct extensive research on a continuing basis to ensure that the products or services being offered are in line with the marketplace. Obviously, this is an expensive and time-consuming process; one that you undoubtedly want to avoid.

Through several easy and inexpensive methods, you can find out everything you want to know about your potential market. But first you need to determine exactly what information you need. It might be population or economic trends, the number of new homes built locally within the last five years, or how many people are active in a particular hobby.

The greater the difficulty, the more glory there is in surmounting it. Skillful pilots gain their reputations from storms and tempests.

Anonymous

The nearest Census Bureau office and your local chamber of commerce are consistently good sources for regional statistics. The reference librarian at the public library can steer you toward other data that will give you the specifics you seek.

The Small Business Administration (SBA) compiles extensive marketing information, in addition to material on operating procedures for specific types of businesses.

Check the *Encyclopedia of Associations* at the library to find the name and address of the advisory board for your industry. Trade boards can provide associates with marketing statistics, management tips, and a wealth of valuable information. Often it only takes a phone call to get more details than you could ever use.

Another excellent source of information on population, income, and sales figures is the annual survey of buying power published by *Sales and Marketing Management Magazine,* which breaks the information down by county and cities in the United States and should be available through the library.

Media Kits and Personal Contact

The advertising departments of local magazines and newspapers undoubtedly have a "media kit" available for potential advertisers, which they will gladly send you upon request. These packets contain a breakdown of their advertising rates and specifications, a description of why advertising with them is to your benefit and, most important, a profile of their readership. A friendly conversation with one of their salespeople should give you a wealth of data.

The merchants from whom you will be buying supplies, equipment, and products are another excellent source. They can give you a good rundown on trends, as well as an overview of current sales figures for their products. Since they are hoping you will eventually use them as a supplier for your business, they will be more than happy to give you free information.

It is, of course, often possible to gauge what the competition is doing and to glean information from them. There are two approaches when talking to people who are soon to be in direct competition. One is to be up-front and honest about your business plans and appeal to their sense of "industry spirit."

Surprisingly, you will find the direct approach works in the majority of cases as most people are genuinely interested in and supportive of others trying to make it in their field. It is better for everyone if "industry" standards are maintained and competitors have a healthy rapport. And, except in extreme situations such as a very small community, there is generally enough business to go around. It shouldn't be difficult to capture your share of the market, especially if you can develop something unique to attract them.

On the other hand, if competitors are less than receptive, it may be necessary to do some detective work to get the information you want.

Focus Groups

If you really want an indepth marketing study, consider gathering together a group of people (family members, a social or church group, or friends) for a focus session to determine if your service will match the needs of the prospective audience. This involves presenting your proposed business idea and creating a question-naire that calls for specific answers from the group members.

Referral Discounts

Here's a way to boost your income that will make your clients happy to promote the business. Offer clients who provide you with the name of a potential customer (or who have someone call you) a discount on billing. If it results in a job, give a 10 percent discount to the referring party.

This method is often used by companies when they are testing new products and, in fact, there are private companies that do nothing but put focus groups together and set up testing sites in stores, shopping malls, and street corners to obtain spontaneous and objective input from potential consumers.

The questions you would want to include on your question-naire would cover such aspects as how often members of the focus group have used a similar service in the past, what they liked about it, what they found to be unsatisfactory, how they feel it could have been improved, whether they would be willing to try another, and vital statistics such as their age, income, and any specifics that relate to your proposed business.

With the temporary help business, the questions might include a breakdown of the top three reasons people in your focus group would consider using your services, what kinds of documents they would normally have typed, and what additional services they would appreciate seeing you offer (editing, proofreading, etc.). This kind of information will give you an immediate edge on the competition when you are ready to start advertising.

Analyzing Your Research

The bottom line in conducting your research is that you want to zero in on information that provides insights on the potential for your business idea before you invest time, money, and energy in setting it up.

If, for example, you were considering starting your temporary help business in a small community, and your focus group information indicated that only 10 percent of the local residents would consider using your service, you would definitely want to reconsider the validity of your concept or figure ways to promote it on a broader scale.

On the other hand, if your marketing research pointed out that 90 percent of the population thought it was a great idea and that 50 percent would have an immediate need for it, the potential for your business would be much greater, and proceeding with the idea would probably guarantee a profitable venture.

Buy an inexpensive notebook to help you keep track of your marketing data. Use a separate page for each category you are researching. The notebook will serve as your personal, ongoing market study to be reviewed and amended as your business grows and the audience you are serving changes.

Plan to update your information as new studies are published (generally an annual event), indicating changes in population,

economy, or buying and spending trends. Most newspapers publish synopses of local, state, and federal studies of this nature, so maintain your notebook as appropriate. You should also reserve several pages to record comments and suggestions from customers once your business is established, which will help you personalize the service to the market and keep you a step ahead of the competition.

Spend as much time as needed to feel comfortable about your marketing project. The important point is that the results of your research are comprehensive enough to provide you with concrete information on who your potential customers are and how you can best reach them.

Review

I have completed my entrepreneurial profile to determine my strengths and weaknesses.

My friends and family have given me additional input based on the profile.

I am aware of the advantages and disadvantages of going into business for myself.

Time is not a problem; I can easily devote the time I'll need to build my business.

The important people in my life are supportive of my decision.

I have analyzed my cash flow to ensure that I can support myself and my family for at least six months or until the business is solvent.

I feel confident about my future as a business owner at this point.

I know what people want as far as my business is concerned.

I have conducted informal studies to determine my potential customers and understand their needs.

I have analyzed the competition, know what they offer, and have a general idea about their success ratio.

I have done my marketing research and know how to get in touch with the audience I want to reach.

I have contacted the trade association for my industry and have accumulated facts and figures regarding the pros and cons of starting my own business.

I feel confident that my service is marketable.

Notes

Target Audience

Publications to Reach Audience

Additional Research Information

7

LOCATION: COMMERCIAL VERSUS HOME-BASED

\mathbf{A}s far as your clients are concerned, it does not matter where you are located. You will mostly be dealing with them by telephone, or you will be making sales calls at their business.

As far as your temps are concerned, it is best to locate in a central business district or an easily accessed area that has good parking nearby. You will want to make it easy for your temps to come to you, as attracting a good number of temps, and keeping them, is essential for your success.

Temps need to come to your office at first for testing, and then they may come by regularly to pick up their paychecks, time slips, and so on.

As far as choosing the city to locate the business, check out your specific market. One temp agency owner who specializes in placing domestic temps said that she knew her business would succeed in Montecito, California, because there is a lot of money there. She determined that domestic temps are a luxury, and it takes rich people to afford them.

It is not feasible to run a temporary help agency out of your home, since you will have many temps coming in and out all day, *unless* you can set up a room as a separate office away from the

regular household. But you do not need a large office or an office with any kind of special features. You can definitely start small. All you will need is space for a desk, typewriter or word processor, and a telephone.

The ideal situation would include a reception area and separate offices or cubicles for interviewing and testing applicants. The interviewees then will have their privacy to take tests and to be interviewed. In addition, this setup allows you to deal with several applicants at one time. For example, while one person is taking a typing test, another could be interviewed.

As you grow and hire employees, such as interviewers and a receptionist, it will become more and more important to have the space to carry out many different activities at one time.

General Guidelines for Commercial Locations

Selecting the right location is vital to the success of your business. The first two factors you must analyze when looking for a commercial location are

1. The community you want to live and/or work in, based on family needs, finances, your preference for a particular area because of health reasons, or the fact that you have an established reputation in a certain area

2. The locations available within that community

These factors are interrelated. You may want to settle down in an area with a limited number of suitable business locations available. Or you may have run across a number of viable sites in several communities or locations, in which case an investigation of each must be conducted, covering each of the following points:

1. *The type of business you are planning to operate.* Remember that retail, wholesale, and service businesses have slightly different requirements as determined by the type of product or service being offered and the market potential in a specific area.

2. *The demographics of the area.* You should find out the number of consumers who want or need your product or

service and are willing and able to pay your price, the median income and employment opportunities, the age ranges of the major population group, and the volume of retail trade and projected expansion data (available from census reports and chamber of commerce business reports accumulated during your market research project).

3. ***Competition.*** You must determine how many other similar establishments are serving the market and how their businesses are going to decide if there is room for your new venture. The best way to do this is by making a list of businesses from the phone book that you feel will be in direct competition and, if feasible, visit their locations at different times of day to observe the activity levels and to talk with employees, who should be willing to answer your questions if you approach them in a friendly way. Often, the same kind of research can be accomplished on the telephone.

4. ***Traffic patterns.*** Is your proposed location close to freeways, major intersections, and/or a central business district? Is there sufficient parking? Is the foot traffic past the location strong and steady enough to guarantee walk-in trade that will generate sales and profits? The ease with which customers can get to your location is a major consideration in terms of success.

5. ***Your image.*** Before you go scouting for locations, decide on the image you want to project, such as quality products at good prices, superior service, and convenience.

6. ***The product or service.*** If, for example, you were planning to sell high priced, state-of-the-art European electronic equipment, it would advisable to locate your business in a mall or on the main street of an economically comfortable community to ensure getting the response you need to survive. Generally, there are specific areas within a marketplace that cater to consumers in specific income brackets and/or occupational groups, i.e., executives, blue-collar workers, students, etc. Consider

your product/service and the projected number of poten-
tial buyers within the community.

7. ***The amount of rent required.*** Locations having the
highest potential of profit through consumer traffic (such
as a prime downtown site or shopping mall, a corner shop,
or a store with good frontage) are more expensive be-
cause competition keeps rents up to the maximum. The
trade-off is an increase in sales and a lower advertising
budget because of the visibility factor.

Retail Locations

The guidelines indicated above are applicable for retail businesses.
Poor location is one of the chief causes of failure among retail
stores, but, on the other hand, the right location can be all it takes
for even a mediocre business to thrive and grow.

Service Businesses

When clients are going to be visiting your place of business, the
same principles of location selection apply as are indicated for
retail. If clients will not be visiting, location selection can be based
on rent, the amount of space needed, and the convenience to you.

Wholesale, Manufacturing, or Mail-Order Businesses

Where you locate a wholesale business depends on your market.
If dealing primarily with local retailers or customers, your location
should be within easy driving distance of your clientele.

However, if most of your business is conducted through the
mail or delivery services, you can base your selection on the best
rent available and the convenience factor for you and your staff.
When choosing a location for your wholesale business, warehous-
ing needs are a vital consideration, as is projected expansion.

Before Signing a Lease

Unless you're planning to purchase the commercial location, rent
your location from a family member or accept a temporary agree-
ment in a location that is for sale. But keep in mind that you will

be required to sign a lease before moving in. The most desirable agreement for you as a new business owner is a one- to two-year lease with a renewal option and a guaranteed rate for rent increases over a five- to ten-year period.

Rent for a commercial location is established either on a flat rate or a percentage basis. Under the flat rate, rent is generally based on the square footage of the shop and on the location or, in some cases, on potential volume. The percentage base involves a base amount of rent plus a prearranged percentage of monthly sales.

Your lease will also cover a number of other points, such as the liabilities and responsibilities of the landlord and of you, the tenant; i.e., who is to pay for utilities, specific repairs, renovations, tax increases, etc.

The lease may contain stipulations about the size of the exterior sign you can erect, hours of operation, insurance coverage, and assignation of the lease to another party (a sublet).

Before signing a lease to set up your business, make sure that electrical lines are adequate enough to handle high-volume usage, that you have rest rooms for employees and/or clients, and that there are convenient parking areas. Also check with the leasing agent to be certain you can make leasehold improvements, e.g., storage shelves, at your discretion as the business warrants it.

It is recommended that you have an attorney review the lease carefully before you sign it to ensure you understand all of the clauses and to serve as a negotiator, if necessary.

Setting Up Your Business at Home

Operating your business from home is appealing. Thousands of successful businesses have been started in a basement, a spare room, or on the kitchen table. It's true that Henry Ford founded the Ford Motor Company in his garage and Jean Nidetch started Weight Watchers in her living room as a support group for friends who wanted to lose weight. Both of these businesses, and many more like them, became successful multimillion-dollar corporations despite humble beginnings.

The Small Business Administration estimates that there are close to twenty million home-based businesses in the United States

today and, of these, more than 30 percent are owned and operated by women.

Starting a home-based business has provided an opportunity for many people who might otherwise never have the chance to become business owners. Women, especially, have discovered that they can build a profitable, satisfying business at home while still being available for their families.

For others, a home-based business is the ticket out of the world of the urban commuter. In fact, a home-based business is the perfect way to try something new to see how it works while still working another job to pay the bills. Once the business has proven itself and is realizing a profit, you can leave the job to devote all your time to your new venture.

Couples often find that investing time and energy in building a business together at home develops stronger relationships in addition to increasing joint income. For the retired and for those with minor physical disabilities, it is a path to staying involved, exploring self-sufficiency, and guaranteeing that there can be a profitable future.

Start-ups Never Change

As with any new business, whether located at home or in a commercial location, it is important to follow the basic guidelines for start-up, including conducting a market survey, drawing up a business plan, setting goals, reviewing capital needs and projected income, developing an advertising campaign, and establishing a professional image.

Advantages of a Home-Based Business

♦ Ability to start your business immediately

♦ Minimal start-up capital needed

♦ No rent or excessive setup charges for utilities

♦ Comfortable working conditions

♦ Reduced wardrobe expenses

♦ No commuting

♦ Tax benefits

♦ Elimination of office politics

♦ Flexibility and independence

♦ Full utilization and recognition of skills

♦ Low risk for trial and error

However, many businesses, such as maid services, can be set up easily in the home, offering a number of advantages for the owner who is just starting out.

Setting up your business at home automatically eliminates up to 75 percent of the start-up costs and responsibilities required for an office or storefront operation. You are, in your home, already making rent or mortgage payments and paying for your own telephone service, insurance, and utilities. (In many instances, a commercial location will require $10,000 just to open the doors with basic leasehold improvements and/or equipment.) In addition, valuable time and energy are saved because you don't have to scout for the location, have utilities installed, and decorate the premises.

Getting Your Feet Wet

A home-based business gives you the opportunity to test the waters with a minimum of risk. This is especially beneficial to first-time entrepreneurs, who may prefer to learn and grow with

the business in the comfort of home without the pressures that operating out of a commercial location often bring.

As a hedge against inflation, the home-based business is a natural. In addition to low start-up, tax deductions for use of a home office and business expenses provide relief from a seemingly endless outflow of cash spent on mortgage or rent payments. You must, however, be aware of the tax laws, which allow deductions only for that part of the home "used exclusively and regularly" for business and limited to a modified net income of the business.

After the business is running smoothly, you will find that the potential to earn money is greater because of reduced overhead. Your production will increase because you have more control over your schedule and fewer of the typical interruptions that arise in a commercial setting. Of course, as with any business arrangement, there are also disadvantages to setting up your business in your home. By recognizing them, however, it is possible to address and minimize the problems before they come up.

Disadvantages of a Home-Based Business

- ◆ Success is based 100 percent on your efforts
- ◆ Difficult to establish solid work habits
- ◆ Difficult to determine competitive rates
- ◆ Limited support system
- ◆ Isolation
- ◆ Limited work space
- ◆ Disruption of personal life
- ◆ Clients are uncomfortable coming to your home
- ◆ Zoning restrictions

Getting to Work

One of the biggest problems faced by home-based entrepreneurs is being able to establish a productive work schedule. There are

different types of interruptions that come up in a home environment, including visits from friends and neighbors, household chores that need to be done, the temptation of television and the daily paper when there is work to be produced, and the fact that there is no one around to spur you on.

A helpful suggestion for getting down to work is to dress in the morning as if you were going out to a regular job. This alone will help you set your priorities for the day.

The best solution, however, is to establish regular working hours at the outset (although you do have the flexibility as a home-based business owner to arrange your schedule around the times you know you are the most productive). If friends want to visit, politely explain to them that you are operating a business that requires your full concentration and arrange a suitable time to get together according to your schedule.

It is also important, if you have family, that they are supportive and willing to arrange their lives as much as possible around your schedule. This can be dealt with through frequent family discussions about what you are doing and how the business operates.

Another difficult area is learning to separate business and pleasure. A home-based business often makes it very easy to work day and night on a project. Again, it is important to allot time for personal activities. The point to remember is that the work will get done much more efficiently if you are relaxed and rested.

It is also a good idea to have the business set up in a separate room or area that can be shut off from your personal living space after working hours. This will more easily enable you to separate work from leisure time.

Home-based business owners often experience feelings of isolation from those in their industry. One way to eliminate this is to join local groups, such as the chamber of commerce and networking groups, and to attend the meetings. Check to see how many members are entrepreneurs, which will give you a built-in support system. By making yourself available to serve on committees, you'll be able to reach into the community and publicize your business for the cost of your involvement.

Reviewing Local Laws

Before getting started, it is important to check that zoning ordinances in your area will allow you to use your home for business purposes. Since zoning ordinances vary from city to city and county to county, it is necessary to contact the planning department of your regional government offices or talk with your attorney to find out what is allowed, based on the type of business, the area to be used within your home, noise control, tax regulations, business signs, and other aspects, as well as if you need a special permit or license to operate.

If you are expecting clients to visit your home for business, it is best to have a separate room set up as an office so that when they do come to discuss your product or service, they won't feel as if they are intruding on a family. If, however, an office is out of the question, make sure you arrange meetings during times when the family is away from home to ensure that there will be no interruptions.

Another option is to go to the client's location when you must have meetings or to offer pickup and delivery service, if applicable. Depending on the business, however, and the quality of your work, client discomfort shouldn't be a major problem, according to a number of home-based business owners we have interviewed.

The number of home-based businesses has increased dramatically over the past few years. The bottom line, as far as the client is concerned, is—and will always be—reliable service and high-quality work provided in a professional atmosphere by a professional person.

God gives every bird its food, but He does not throw it in the nest.

J.G. Holland

The benefits of a home-based business to the beginning entrepreneur can mean the difference between working for someone else or turning a dream into reality. The key element, as with any business, is motivation, a needed product or service, careful plan-

ning, and the desire to succeed. Just knowing that the expenses of establishing a business in a commercial location are alleviated by setting up a home-based enterprise is enough to push you forward to success, one small step after another.

Utilities and Phone

The home-based business has an additional advantage: Your phone line and utilities are already in place. Any additional equipment is easy to obtain from your utility carriers because you already have an established payment history.

Single-line telephone systems are adequate for most small businesses, but when your business outgrows a single-line system, you'll need a multiline system enabling you to accept several calls simultaneously and switch between lines.

Regardless of whether you need a single line or a multiline telephone system, some options are now available when choosing equipment.

Programmable memory allows automatic storage and instant dialing of phone numbers by pressing a button or entering a code.

Automatic redial reconnects the last number dialed, in some cases redialing at specific intervals until the call goes through.

Speed dialing allows you to quickly access frequently dialed numbers by using a one- to four-digit code.

Call waiting is especially useful for businesses with single lines, allowing you to take incoming calls while putting the original caller on hold.

Conference calling is often a related feature of call waiting, allowing you to simultaneously speak with two or more parties at different locations.

Call forwarding routes incoming calls to a preprogrammed phone number at another location.

Cordless phones are especially useful for the home business, allowing you to make or accept calls from any location in the house. Because cordless phones vary in quality, it's strongly recommended that you research the market before buying.

Speaker phones allow you to carry on conversations without the constraint of holding a receiver. One of the main benefits is

that you can accomplish other tasks while waiting on hold. They're also useful for note taking and similar chores during business conversations.

Voice mail is a combination answering, routing, and messaging system that can help cut front-office payroll costs (if you have a staff) while maximizing efficiency. Customers dialing a voice mail number are greeted by a recorded message and given a menu of options: direct-dialing employees in other departments, leaving messages for one or more individuals, receiving additional recorded information, and using the voice-mail system with a rotary-dial phone.

The cost of voice mail has been scaled down dramatically in recent years and is now available for small or even one-person businesses, presenting a first-class image while actually saving you money (not only in payroll costs but in avoiding potential lost revenues from unanswered or misdirected calls).

Long-Distance Carriers

Whether you're a one-person, home-based operation or an expanding business in a commercial location, long-distance service is, of course, essential.

The host of carriers competing for your long-distance dollar, their conflicting claims, and a wide range of services can bewilder the small business owner trying to make a choice.

When deciding which carrier to use for your business, consider the following:

♦ Areas of the country and the world that you will most frequently be calling

♦ Monthly amount you anticipate spending on long-distance calls

♦ Time of day you'll be making most of your calls

♦ Seasonal calling patterns

♦ Whether you'll be dealing only with clients statewide (a regional WATS line would be a cost-effective choice)

In addition, read the various carriers' promotional information carefully. Does the carrier you're considering charge start-up or installation fees or a flat monthly fee? If the latter, will you meet the carrier's minimum usage requirements and are the services offered worth the monthly charge?

Other factors to consider include available volume discounts based on usage and dedicated lines giving you exclusive access to a telecommunications network.

800 Numbers

Businesses that market products and services regionally or nationally have found the 800 number to be one of their most effective marketing tools. Customers who might not otherwise pay for a long-distance call now pick up the phone without hesitation—and frequently wind up requesting further information about services or making hefty credit card purchases.

Though 800 numbers can pay for themselves thousands of times over, the installation fees, service charges, and usage fees can be expensive. Consider carefully whether the potential costs outweigh the benefits. An alternative is the localized 800 number, available for small, highly targeted geographic areas. Consult your phone company's service representative for further information.

Review

If setting up my business at home, I have

Checked with the city and county offices in my area regarding required licenses and permits and zoning regulations for the home office

Set aside a room or an area in my home that will be used exclusively for my business

Checked prices on storage units and worktables

Planned a layout that I feel will work well for the location and my storage, display, and office needs

Have a separate telephone line and answering machine, or contracted with an answering service

Set up a separate business bank account

Informed friends and family of my business routine and specific working hours to reduce interruptions and distractions

If setting up in a commercial location, I have

Investigated rental rates for the area I am interested in

Checked traffic flow, parking, and foot traffic around my proposed location

Determined that my business is compatible with others

Talked with my prospective landlord about improvements, maintenance, and rent increases

Had my lawyer check the rental agreement and any local zoning regulations

Secured the necessary operating licenses and permits from the city and/or county

Notes

Key Points

Possible Locations

Size and Floor Plan Considerations

8

START-UP BASICS

Having decided that you are ready and able to accept the challenge of starting your own business, it is necessary to take a look at your overall financial picture. Even if you have a healthy savings account, or feel you can start your business with a minimal capital investment, diagnosing your personal financial situation will help you determine ongoing expenses.

The easiest way to estimate exactly how much money you will need to get your business started and to cover expenses, including personal living expenses for the first six months, is to prepare a *Cash Flow Statement* and a *Projected Expense Statement.* Samples are provided in this chapter.

Preparing the Projected Expense Statement will give you a fairly accurate picture of what it will cost to open the doors and will indicate how much income you must generate to realize a profit. Another advantage of creating these charts early in the game is that two of the required documents will already be prepared when you want to explore funding options, then you will only need to update them.

The first step in examining your financial situation is to ask yourself the following questions:

1. Do I generally pay my bills on time or do I wait until my creditors start sending me collection notices?

2. Have I regularly reconciled my bank statement so I know how much money I have in my checking account at any given time?

3. Is my philosophy "If I've got it, I spend it" or do I carefully plan how I am going to use my income?

4. Have I ever developed a personal budget so I know how much money is coming in, how much is going out, and what I have left over?

These are important aspects of your financial personality that will be helpful to understand when running your business. As your business and subsequent involvement with financial matters grow, it will be vital that you have a handle on your philosophy about money. And there is no time like in the beginning, when your business concept is being formed, to start learning.

The Cash Flow Statement

Use the Cash Flow Statement at the end of this chapter to determine your personal living expenses for the past three to six months to help you gauge what you will need to survive during the early stages of your business.

The easiest way to complete the statement is to use your checkbook register or sales receipts as research tools. If your expenses are relatively consistent from month to month, you should be able to get an overview by analyzing one month. A more accurate picture will emerge if you break down income and expenses for three to six months to account for periodic payments, such as taxes, insurance, and seasonal spending.

Using the samples provided, fill in the amounts in each category from your checkbook register or receipts. Use a separate sheet for every month that you are analyzing. For miscellaneous spending, a standard calculation is 5 percent of monthly income. Add up each month's expenses, total them all, and then divide that figure by the number of months you are analyzing. This will give you an average monthly expense figure.

Follow the same procedure for income. You can then subtract your expenses from your income to see where you stand. If you have computed your figures accurately, you might run across a few surprises. It isn't unusual to discover that we spend more money than we realize, often on unnecessary purchases. You may be able to see some areas where you can cut back.

The main points, however, are that you now know

1. How much or whether you can afford to invest your own money in your new business

2. What it costs for you to live comfortably, which will help you set income goals for the business

Start-up Costs

Every business owner has specific standards about how he or she wants to run the operation. One person may feel perfectly comfortable waiting to order business cards until there is a profit. Another wouldn't dream of opening the doors without cards, brochures, and letterhead already printed.

You will have your own ideas about what you need before opening your business. Then you must find out what it will cost and, if at all possible, prepare the *Start-up Costs Worksheet* at the end of this chapter.

It is also advisable to figure how much it will cost to run the business for three to six months, using the sample Projected Expense Statement. A six-month projection should give you the opportunity to determine your profits down the line.

Preparing the Start-up Costs Worksheet and Projected Expense Statement involves conducting some research. For example, to estimate the cost of business cards or letterhead stationery, contact several printers or copy shops in your area and obtain quotes. Call the local newspaper for prices on different types of ads, including display and classified.

An insurance agent will be able to give you an estimate on liability coverage. Check with the telephone company for information and rates on installing a phone line.

You can also start to shop around to find the best prices on office supplies, equipment, and other materials needed to conduct business.

After you have completed your research, incorporate the information on the blank charts. Obviously, some of your figures, such as those for telephone expenses, will be guesstimated. However, the final figure will give you a good idea of start-up and operational costs for the first six months.

Utilizing the same theory, you can develop a *Projected Income Statement* (worksheet not provided), drawing from industry figures available through your trade association or other research sources. This would include all income realized from cash sales, collection on outstanding invoices, credit card sales, and miscellaneous income. By subtracting your total expenses from total income, you will get a clear picture of projected profit or loss.

All of these statements will be requested by loan officers, venture capitalists, and the Small Business Administration if and when you apply for a loan. This kind of paperwork is required to ensure that you have basic business knowledge, a commendable track record, and are serious about your venture. You will also be required to fill out a personal financial statement, available through the lending institution, especially if you are the sole owner or a general partner in the business.

General Office Equipment

Adding machine. Many computers include a built-in calculator and keypad. The advantage of an adding machine is that it provides a paper record of your figures, while a calculator provides only a temporary display.

Answering machines. Answering machines are an inexpensive way to ensure that your clients can leave a message when you're away from the office. Although there are still people who feel uncomfortable talking to a machine, anyone with an important message will overcome that discomfort, especially if your outgoing message is friendly. And with the popularity of answering machines increasing, the general public is becoming more used to them and less likely to hang up. In fact some prospective clients may be highly annoyed if you do not have a machine to take their

messages when you are out, since it is a waste of their time to keep calling you back in hopes of catching you in the office.

Machines are available in a wide range of prices. Top-of-the-line models may feature voice-activated messaging without time constraints, remote access codes that allow you to call in to your own line for messages when you're away, and a message counter featuring the time and date messages were left.

Bookcase and inventory shelving system. You might find yourself building a small library of reference materials, as well as holding on to various trade publications. An inexpensive bookcase is a good way to keep everything in one place.

You will also find that your printed matter (brochures, business cards, letterhead, order forms, billing forms, etc.) takes up quite a bit of space. Bookcases or shelving units will keep these items organized.

Computer. In these days of computerization, it is a necessity to have a computer to test employees' computer skills. A great number of clients will expect temporary employees who can handle word processing tasks. A computer also makes inventory control and customer file maintenance ten times more efficient. You can find more details in Chapter 9, "Computerizing Your Office."

Desk and chair. You're going to spend a significant amount of time either sitting in front of your computer or sitting at a desk doing paperwork and making telephone calls. Therefore, it's extremely important that you invest in the right desk and chair.

Not only will the wrong furniture give you back and neck aches, studies have proven that it can cause extreme fatigue and a decrease in overall productivity.

Depending on your height, you will want your computer keyboard desktop to be about twenty-six inches from the ground; writing surfaces are generally thirty inches high, so you might want to look for an adjustable computer desk that accommodates both tasks comfortably.

Even more important is the chair. It should provide support for the base of the spine, a backrest no higher than your shoulder blades, and a seat that can be raised or lowered easily. A solid seat and rounded cushion to prevent the restriction of blood flow in the legs is recommended. The lumbar support and armrests should

also be adjustable since everyone's body is proportioned differently. The best way to find the chair you need is to visit an office furniture store and try out several until you find one that feels comfortable.

Filing cabinet. An absolutely essential item is a filing cabinet to keep all of your papers in order. It is not enough to keep a ledger of income and expenses. You must also save all invoices, receipts, canceled checks, copies of work orders, and lists of customers' names, etc. Of extreme importance is that you must keep payroll records on all of your temporary workers.

Of course, much of this information can be input and maintained directly on your computer, but there is still a need for a simple filing system for "hard copies" and those paper odds and ends that must be saved for income tax purposes. All you need is a standard two- or four-drawer filing cabinet to begin with. Be sure, however, that you don't fall into the trap of buying your filing cabinet through a discount department store–typically these are substandard brands and frequently are not properly weighted. We've heard more than one story about drawers falling out or the whole cabinet falling over on some unsuspecting person.

Telephones. In a commercial location, getting a business telephone will be one of the first steps in setting up your business. If starting your business at home, you will likely be using your home telephone. However, plan to install a separate business line as soon as possible to maintain your professional image.

There is nothing more annoying to a client than being unable to get through because the personal line is tied up or having a child answer a "business" phone, no matter how carefully they are trained to answer courteously. The advantage of a business line is that you can hook up an answering machine to intercept calls that come in after your established business hours.

Although it is still possible to rent telephones through certain telephone companies, the best bet is to buy your own. They are inexpensive, come in a variety of styles and colors, and are generally covered by a warranty.

Typewriter. This is mandatory, so that you can test typing skills and speed.

Specialized Supplies

Specialized supplies include

♦ Test forms

♦ Applications

♦ Contracts

♦ Time cards

Costs vary widely for these supplies, and you must call around and compare prices to get the best deal. Many of the forms can be purchased preprinted, but they are often very expensive.

Tara Gordon has found a creative way around paying the high prices. "Some preprinted forms, which include contracts for temporary agencies, applications, and so forth, can be costly," she says. "I have found it is less expensive to get a hold of a sample of those forms, copy down the information, and have it printed up myself."

Gordon said she took seminars on interviewing from her local college and used sample forms to create basic typing and spelling tests. She added that word processing is in great demand for temps, and that it can be tested without actually having the equipment. Instead, many agencies test such skills on paper, using written tests that outline the particulars of specific computer programs.

Start-up Costs Worksheet

Furniture: Purchase price $_____

 Down payment required $_____

Fixtures: Purchase price _____

 Down payment required _____

Equipment: Purchase price _____

 Down payment required _____

Installation and delivery costs _____

Decorating & leasehold improvements _____

Deposits: Utilities and rent _____

Fees: Legal, accounting, consulting, etc. _____

Licenses & permits _____

Starting inventory _____

Supplies _____

Printing _____

Initial advertising & promotion _____

Miscellaneous _____

Total Start-up Expense $_____

Less Available Start-up Capital $_____

Total Amount Needed $_____

Projected Expense Statement

Months	1st	2nd	3rd	4th	5th	6th
Rent						
Utilities						
Telephone						
Insurance						
Professional services						
Taxes & licenses						
Advertising						
Office supplies						
Office equipment						
Inventory						
Business auto expense						
Travel expense						
Entertainment						
Dues & subscriptions						
Salaries						
Owner's draw						
Loan payments						
Interest payments						
Miscellaneous						
TOTALS						

Cash Flow Statement
Month of _____

Income		Expenses	
Wages	$_____	Rent or mortgage	$_____
Miscellaneous	$_____	Auto loan	$_____
		Gas & auto repairs	$_____
TOTAL	$_____	Auto insurance	$_____
		Life insurance	$_____
		Medical insurance	$_____
Savings	$_____	Homeowner's insurance	$_____
		Taxes	$_____
Credit Line	$_____	Loan payments	$_____
		Food: At home	$_____
		Food: Dining out	$_____
Home Equity	$_____	Telephone	$_____
		Utilities	$_____
		Household repairs, etc.	$_____
		Medical bills	$_____
		Credit card payments	$_____
		Interest expense	$_____
		Clothing/dry cleaning	$_____
		Travel	$_____
		Miscellaneous	$_____
		Savings	$_____
		TOTAL	$_____

9

COMPUTERIZING YOUR OFFICE

In choosing your computer, the following criteria should be considered: the speed of the overall system and, related to this, the on-board (resident) software that drives the computer and its compatibility with other software packages that you may need down the road.

In addition, you'll want to check the system's upgrade capability (the ease with which you can upgrade components when the manufacturer offers new or revised product lines); and the system's overall compatibility with hardware offered by competing manufacturers.

Once you've decided on your business applications and software needs, the next step is buying the hardware. Hardware comprises not only the computer (central processing unit or CPU, monitor, mouse, and keyboard), but, peripherals (printers, modems, etc.) and add-ons (such as fax and graphics boards).

In a constantly changing computer market, your best bets include reading the appropriate computer journals, calling manufacturers' customer service departments, and—most important—comparison shopping.

Hardware prices can vary widely from store to store, so it literally pays to shop around. Talk to a variety of salespeople, but don't let them talk you into a purchase. It's your decision, and it's

too important to let it be dictated by a commission-hungry pitch-man. Take your time, then base your decision first on need, then on price. A low price is no bargain if you walk away with a computer whose memory or other functions are inadequate or—worse yet—incompatible with your software needs.

In selecting hardware, your main considerations center on

1. Current and future business applications
2. Software requirements
3. Necessary peripherals
4. Price

Term Warfare

The first challenge in hunting for hardware is surviving the initial cross fire of computer-speak. If you can master a few simple terms (and can type), you'll likely master the computerized home environment.

First, a few basics. The core of a computer system is the central processing unit, which among other things interacts with software. Virtually all CPUs contain at least one floppy disk drive, designed for either $5\frac{1}{4}$ or 3.5-inch magnetic disks on which text, graphics, and additional data are stored. The main storage area, however, is the system's internal or "fixed" drive, also known as the hard disk, which offers increased storage capacity.

Storage capacity refers to the amount of data that can be saved and is measured in terms of bytes or characters (each alphabetic letter, number, or punctuation mark represents a char-acter). Under one million characters, floppy-disk storage is meas-ured in kilobytes, signified with a capital K: An 800K disk thus can store 800,000 characters. Storage of one-million-plus characters is measured in megabytes, signified with a capital M or MB. A 30MB hard drive thus can store up to thirty million bytes of data.

In addition to storing data (broken down into files), floppy and hard drives store and load software, allowing immediate access to a variety of programs.

A low price is no bargain if you walk away with a computer whose memory or other functions are inadequate or incompatible with your software.

The second element in the computer system is the monitor, or screen, available either in monochrome (black and white) or color. If you will be doing a lot of graphics work, a color monitor is essential. A mouse or other pointer device is necessary for most of the applications you will be using. There is also the keyboard, with a layout similar to that of a typewriter. Placement of function keys and the touch or feel of the keyboard are the major differences between models.

Next, you must consider peripherals—most commonly the printer and modem. Printers come in three forms: dot matrix, ink jet, and laser.

Modems transmit and receive computer data over telephone lines, connecting you electronically with the outside world— whether a print shop down the street or a client in Europe.

Modems usually are categorized by their transmission (or baud) rate, measured in bits (characters) per second (bps). Baud rates are typically 1200, 2400, and 9600, but more commonly range upward of 14400. Modems of 2400 baud and higher are recommended for long documents. The higher the baud rate, the faster the transmission time and thus the lower your phone bill, since transmission time is billed as telephone time. In addition, there is the fax modem, which turns your telephone into a data retrieval/transmission center.

Finding the Right System

The leading edge computer market is divided into two segments: the Apple Macintosh and IBM compatibles, the latter now dominated by Windows—a graphical user interface similar to that of the Macintosh. Here's where things get both interesting and a little confusing. The growth of desktop publishing has resulted in a flood of products, and it can be difficult to make your equipment choices. The choice does, however, essentially boil down to two

general computer environments: the Apple Macintosh or Microsoft Windows for the IBM PC and its clones.

What makes one better or worse than the other? That decision must be left in the hands of consumers. Each camp has its loyal followers. To set your business up, you'll need to decide what system you personally like best. Here is some general comparative information about each system.

	Macintosh	Windows
Ease of Use	Slightly better	
Ease of Learning New Software	Slightly better	
Graphics Capabilities	Comparable	Comparable
Price of Hardware		Considerably lower
Availability of Hardware		Slightly better
Availability and Cost of Service		Considerably better
Price of Software	Comparable	Comparable
Availability of Quality Software	Comparable	Comparable
Price of Peripherals	Comparable	Comparable
Availability of Peripherals	Comparable	Comparable
Compatibility With Other Businesses	Depends on market segment	Depends on market segment

Instead of outlining all of the available hardware (something that would fill the heftiest of computer magazines), we'll concentrate on the variables that you should consider prior to making a purchase decision.

Keep in mind, however, that you don't have to buy new. You can purchase good late-model systems through computer rental stores (leasing with an option to buy), as well as through used computer outlets and private parties.

Computer Shopping Checklist

♦ Will the computer handle the software programs you've selected, as well as the programs you eventually may need?

♦ How much memory do the software programs require, and does the system need to be expanded to handle them?

♦ What will it cost to expand the system, if necessary?

♦ Is the storage capacity of the hard drive adequate?

♦ How much setup space is required for the computer, printer, and other equipment?

♦ Is the operating system user-friendly, with easy-to-use commands and a comprehensive instruction manual?

♦ What assistance or technical support does the hardware manufacturer provide?

♦ Is the monitor an adequate size and resolution for your needs?

♦ What does the basic system price include (monitor, additional software, etc.)?

♦ What are the terms and length of the warranty, and to what extent is labor included?

♦ What kind of supplemental service contract is available? What will it cost on a monthly or annual basis?

♦ Does the dealer offer ongoing support?

♦ What is the quality of printer output?

♦ How fast and loud is the printer?

♦ Is the dealer willing to put a quote in writing for comparison shopping?

♦ Is financing available through the manufacturer or dealer? At what interest rate?

♦ Is a leasing program available? Can you purchase the
equipment at the end of the term? At what price?

Printers

Here we offer a quick roundup of the leading laser, dot-matrix, and
ink-jet printers. Shop around for the best deal.

Laser. Laser printers work on a principle similar to photo-
copiers. The image from the document stored in your computer is
transferred to a drum by a laser beam. The drum then lays an
electrostatic charge on the paper that attracts toner into the areas
to be printed. The images are set in a series of minute dots that
look like solid lines to the naked eye. Printer resolution is measured
in dots-per-inch (dpi). The higher the resolution the sharper the
image. Laser printer resolution is typically 300, 600, 1000, or 1200
dpi. Printers with higher resolution will generally cost more and
print more slowly than their lower dpi counterparts. Laser printers
have become increasingly affordable in recent years.

Dot Matrix. These printers produce characters composed of
hundreds of dots and are popular choices for the budget-conscious
who don't require high-resolution printing capabilities.

Ink jet. These printers produce pages of text or graphics by
spraying fine jets of ink on the paper to form characters made up
of many dozens of dark black dots. Ink-jet output is often confused
with that of low resolution laser printers. For this reason an ink-jet
printer is a good compromise between the high resolution and high
cost of lasers and the rough low resolution of dot-matrix printers.

Base your hardware purchases on current and future
applications, needed software, available peripherals,
and, of course, price.

Laptops and Notebooks

These lightweight, battery-powered computers can be used as
standalone systems or as add-ons to your home computer, in both

cases providing system access at remote locations—from the back seat of a limo or from a 747 at 30,000 feet.

CD-ROMs

This stands for compact disc read-only memory. It is important to remember that CD-ROMs do not replace hard drives and other storage media because you cannot save your own files to them. (Rewritable CD systems are available, but they are extremely expensive.) Instead, they are used as a means of storing huge amounts of ready-made data, including software applications. They are capable of storing 150,000 pages of text per CD as well as complex graphics and sounds. For this reason they are used to store everything from downloadable fonts to 60-million-word dictionaries to encyclopedias that allow users to listen and view as well as read. CD-ROMs are standard equipment on a number of systems and are now available at an increasingly reasonable cost.

Additional Accessories

Surge suppressors prevent damage to your equipment when there is a fluctuation in voltage. Basically a long strip or box with several power outlets and an on/off switch, they are well worth the minimal investment of less than $50, especially if you live in an area where power spikes or surges are common. You should note, however, that a surge suppressor will not protect unsaved data in the event of a power failure. For that you need an uninterruptible power supply (UPS). You should also be wary of power strips that are not surge protectors. They often look similar, but their only function is to increase the number of outlets. Some surge suppressors come with guarantees that reimburse you for equipment that is damaged by power surges while you are using the suppressor.

Computer and printer covers protect your equipment from dust, which can sneak into the disk drives and under the keys to create problems. They cost an average of $10 to $20 each.

Screen filters reduce glare from windows or lights that reflect off the computer screen and into your eyes, causing eye-strain and headaches. Although a lower level of light is required

for computer input than when working with a typewriter or writing by hand, it's sometimes impossible to prevent glare from a window. For less than $25, you can buy a mesh or plastic screen filter that will fit over the screen.

Disk storage boxes come in a variety of styles and sizes. Generally made of plastic, they not only allow you to keep your library of disks in one convenient place, they also help protect the disks from electromagnetic fields, which can alter and even erase data from disks. You do this by keeping your disks in the box and keeping the box at least three feet away from electronic equipment (such as telephones, calculators, TVs, and stereos).

Shop Carefully

Again, we can't stress enough that it pays to shop carefully. Computer systems can range from below $1,000 to well over $5,000, with many of the lower-priced systems offering all the power and speed you'll need. It's very easy to overspend on technology that you won't really require and is available at a lower price on less expensive models.

Read the leading hardware and software computer magazines and comparison shop at a variety of stores. Also, as mentioned earlier, there's a good chance you'll be able to find a perfectly good previously owned system at a very reasonable price, particularly in light of recent hardware upgrades inducing users to trade up. Check the classifieds and local computer users groups for good buying opportunities.

Mail Order

The same principle applies with mail-order computer houses that advertise in computer magazines. It is possible to save hundreds of dollars buying brand-new systems from mail-order outlets, and you can also buy components.

In either case, do some preliminary research before buying. To the extent possible, know what you're getting.

Financing and Leasing

Many of the major computer manufacturers offer their own financing packages, and major computer hardware stores do as well. Of course, monthly payments are required and, in some instances, interest rates may be above those you could obtain through a personal or business loan. Here, too, it pays to comparison shop to be sure you get the best financing available.

Leasing can be an advantage, since it offers the opportunity to trade in one computer for an upgraded model down the line. You may also have the option of buying the hardware at the end of the term for a preset price. Leasing is discussed in more detail at the end of this chapter.

Back-up Service and Support

As with any electronic device, computers break down and need to be repaired. This can be costly, not only for parts and service but in lost production time. Therefore, be sure any new system you're planning to buy has a good warranty and has a service contract available. (In some cases, used computer stores also offer limited warranties, so be sure to ask when shopping the market.)

New system warranties vary greatly in duration. Any warranty or service contract should cover both parts and labor. One drawback, no matter how good the warranty, is that you'll be required to ship the computer to the service center, perhaps at your own expense. If possible, try to have the dealer sign a statement covering the cost of shipping if the system needs service within the warranty period. Also, ask whether loaners are provided while your system is being repaired.

Service or maintenance contracts may seem like a heavy expense when you've just laid out hundreds and perhaps thousands of dollars on a new system. However, in the event that you need to have major work done—replacing a disk drive, for example—you'll be thankful you made the investment.

Equipment Buying: New or Used?

You can buy new or used equipment from dealers and independent sellers. Or, if you don't mind rummaging through other people's lives, you can find incredible bargains on supplies and equipment at garage sales, swap meets, thrift shops run by charitable organizations, or auctions. Often, it is well worth the time involved because the savings can be significant.

Before investing money, do your homework. Talk with other business owners to find out which brand of equipment they use and why they prefer it over other choices on the market. This will help you make the best decision based on your needs and budget.

Also, talk with independent dealers who carry a broad line of similar types of equipment. They can give you insights on maintenance, longevity, service contracts, and prices.

They will also be able to tell you when to expect a drop in price for the item you are interested in, although you can count on seeing sales on major equipment such as computers and other big-ticket items at store openings and during special sales.

Cash or Credit?

Unless you are planning to pay cash for an equipment purchase, you will either make a down payment and set up a payment schedule with the dealer or take out a loan with the bank. With interest rates for some bank loans currently running at about 10 to 12 percent, you might be able to find a dealer who is willing to handle the financing at a lower rate.

Although this method is a less effective way of establishing your credit, it will serve to get the business going. Another advantage is that if you should find yourself in a tight cash-flow situation at any time, a private dealer/lender with whom you have a personal relationship is much more likely to be flexible...without charging you a penalty for a late payment.

Looking for Bargains

There are many ways to save money buying equipment and supplies, generally through third-party vendors and mail-order

sources. Apple and IBM equipment is sold only through authorized dealers, while IBM clones and third-party peripherals are available everywhere from small stores to mail-order businesses run by electronics whizzes who make their own computers and accessories.

A word of caution here: You need reliable equipment that is backed up by warranty. Whatever your decision on which brand to buy, make sure you are protected with a company that stands behind what it sells.

Shopping around is the only way to get the best deal on equipment and software. If you live in a small town, buy a newspaper for the nearest big city and look for computer ads.

Buying Used Equipment

When buying used equipment from a dealer, the chances of it being in working condition are generally pretty good. Dealers have a reputation to uphold and will stand behind their merchandise, especially if they are firmly established in the community. There are, however, several ways you can scout around to ensure that the one you decide to work with is reputable.

♦ Find a store with membership in the local chamber of commerce. Although this is not an iron-clad guarantee, it does indicate the store owner's interest in following business standards established within the community.

♦ If the dealer also sells new equipment, it is highly likely that much of the used equipment has been traded in by people who are upgrading. You may be able to get an excellent deal on an item that has been carefully maintained by the former owner.

♦ If there is a service department on the premises, you can be assured that used equipment has been reconditioned before being put on sale. It also increases your chances of getting fast, inexpensive, and reliable service if needed at a later date.

♦ Used equipment dealers realize that it is not always easy to find a buyer and should be willing to work with you.

Shopping around will give you an idea of average prices and will give you the information you need to negotiate. If the dealer won't work with you, keep looking.

♦ Know the terms of the warranty. Even used equipment should be covered for a short time for parts and labor, especially if it has been overhauled or reconditioned.

♦ Ask the dealer if he or she is willing to agree to offer a trade-in allowance on the item you are buying when you decide to upgrade. Of course there will be stipulations based on wear and tear and time; however, the dealer should be willing to consider it.

♦ Contact your local Better Business Bureau to see if any complaints have been made about the dealer.

Buyer Beware

There are other ways to find and buy used equipment, but it falls into the realm of "buyer beware." If you choose to deal with private parties through the classified ads or with auctioneers selling off the inventory of a bankrupt business, you must be willing to take a chance. Although the prices will be easy on your budget, the cost of repairing a malfunctioning machine could result in a long-term drain on your profits.

This is not to say that there aren't good opportunities out there. The secret is to know what you are looking for and to have a good idea of how it should work. Do your research by visiting with reliable used-equipment dealers before you start looking.

Ask a private party how long they have owned the equipment, why it is being sold, and if there are any repair bills that you can look at. Trust your intuition in this kind of situation; if the party seems truly interested in providing you with as much information as possible, chances are the equipment is as claimed. If you're told it needs a new part, for example, find out what the replacement part costs and ask if that amount could be deducted from the selling price.

Ask a private party how long they have owned the equipment, why it is being sold, and if there are any repair bills that you can look at.

When you go to see the equipment, make sure it runs. Test it out, if possible, and measure it to make sure it will fit into the space you have available. Also, see whether you can move it yourself or will have to arrange transportation.

Before buying the equipment try to find out if there is a servicing outlet nearby or if you must send away for parts, which can be time-consuming and costly, especially when it comes to older models.

Occasionally you will run across an individual who is making payments on a piece of equipment still under warranty. This can be a great deal for you since he or she will probably accept a small amount of cash and let you take over the payments. Be sure to transfer ownership in writing to prevent complications if you need service under the warranty.

Auctions

Auctions are an excellent way to get equipment and supplies at good prices. Watch the business and classified sections of the newspaper for ads about upcoming auctions. The ad will include dates, the reason for the auction (liquidation or bankruptcy), location, time, and a partial list of items. In most cases there will be a preview, enabling potential buyers to view the merchandise before the bidding begins. Take advantage of the preview to inspect and select the equipment you want to bid on. A fee will be required for a bidder registration number, which is held up when you make a bid so the auctioneer's spotters know who has purchased a particular item.

There are two rules to remember at auctions:

1. Cash or a personal check for the full purchase amount must be paid on the day of the auction.

2. Don't move your hands or make significant gestures during bidding or you might find that you have purchased something you didn't want.

Leasing Equipment

Leasing is defined as a long-term agreement between two parties for the use of a specific item. The person who leases is known as the lessee, while the owner of the item is referred to as the lessor.

Despite the fact that you do not own the equipment when you lease, and so cannot take advantage of depreciation on it for tax purposes, there are still many benefits for the beginning business owner.

Leasing lets you try out a piece of equipment for a given period of time to determine if it is the best product for your needs. Although you are locked in to the terms of the lease, most lessors are flexible.

Know What You Need

Of course, the best way to enter into a lease is to be absolutely clear about what you expect the equipment to do for you. The service representative from the leasing company is well-versed in tailoring equipment to the customer, so do not hesitate to ask questions about capabilities.

Most lessors offer good maintenance contracts, as they want to protect their equipment. Check to see what parts and/or labor are covered before signing the lease. The lessor should also be willing to provide technical advice at no charge, to offer installation and setup of the equipment, and to provide training, if required.

Payments can be arranged to fit your budgetary needs on a monthly, semiannual, or annual basis. This gives you the freedom to schedule payments for peak cash-flow periods. You can also

negotiate the rates and length of the lease to keep monthly operating expenses at a minimum.

Conditional Sales Agreement

Under the provisions of a conditional sales agreement, you become the owner of the leased goods from the agreement date. At the end of the lease period, you are required to purchase the item for a preestablished price. This is often referred to as a balloon payment and should be agreed upon by you and the lessor prior to your signing the lease.

The conditional sales agreement, unlike most other leasing contracts, gives you the tax advantage of claiming depreciation on equipment. Depreciation refers to the decrease in the value of an asset because of wear and tear over a period of time.

You are entitled to deduct depreciation from your income tax based on the value when new, the estimated life of the item, and the value at the end of that estimated life. It is best to work with your accountant on determining depreciation of fixed assets.

There is seldom a down payment, other than the first month's lease amount, required on a leased item, since leasing is generally 100 percent financed for the terms of the agreement. This frees your start-up or working capital for other uses.

True Lease Agreements

You can write off lease payments on your income tax, but only if you have a true lease contract. Under a true lease, the lessor owns the equipment at all times during the contract period. If you decided, at the end of the lease, that you wanted to buy the equipment, you would have to pay whatever purchase price was decided by the lessor.

Financial Lease

The financial lease covers a period that does not extend beyond the estimated life of the equipment. Payments must be made as stipulated on the date due and made consistently to the end of the lease. It usually puts the responsibility and cost of maintenance on the lessee.

Operating Lease

The operating lease generally requires the lessor to handle maintenance of the equipment. It offers the option of canceling the lease, but only if a cancellation clause has been included at the negotiating stage.

The most important aspects of leasing are the terms outlined in the formal lease. Have the lessor draw up a proposal for you, based on everything you have discussed in an initial meeting. If you have any trouble understanding the terms of the proposal, have your accountant review it with you. In fact, it is a definite advantage to have the final lease agreement checked by your attorney or accountant before you sign it.

Your Lease Agreement

Your lease agreement should include

◆ The length of the contract in months or years

◆ The rate you are to be charged, which is usually a percentage of the total purchase price computed on a monthly rate

◆ Your payment schedule

◆ A purchase option, if applicable, at the end of the lease

◆ A renewal option, if applicable, which allows you to carry the lease over for an additional period of time

◆ A cancellation agreement in the event you want or need to cancel the lease

◆ Maintenance stipulations (who pays for parts and labor)

◆ Substitution options if updated equipment is introduced and you want to take advantage of improvements

◆ Any provisions particular to the lease, including tax allowances for depreciation, insurance liability in case of loss or damage, and your responsibilities in reporting a move or other major change

Whether you decide to borrow, buy new equipment, find good used equipment, or lease, be sure to get exactly what you need to keep

costs to a minimum. This is especially important during the early stages of your business when cash is tight. You can always upgrade or add to your equipment inventory as profits increase.

Notes

Key Points

Personal Thoughts

Additional Research

10

PROFESSIONAL BACKUP

From the start-up stage and as your business continues to grow and prosper, you will need the assistance of several professionals, including a lawyer, an accountant, and an insurance agent.

The best way to find a professional is, according to the majority of business owners, through personal recommendations from other entrepreneurs, especially those in similar businesses as yours, and from friends or relatives. The most important factor is that the person doing the recommending understand exactly what you will need from the professional you will be hiring.

For example, your cousin's divorce lawyer is probably not as well suited to helping you draw up a partnership agreement as the attorney a friend used for help with incorporating his business.

Before making a decision, talk to several recommended professionals until you find someone who can best satisfy your needs for the business as outlined below and who has a fee structure you can afford.

Equally important: Your choice should be someone you feel comfortable with, especially during periods when you find yourself having to call several times a week to resolve a problem or complete a specific task.

In many cases, because attorneys and accountants often work on a particular business matter in conjunction with one

another, the attorney you select may be able to suggest an account-
ant who can properly service your business, or vice versa.

If you're planning to hire an attorney or an accountant, you
should start interviewing likely candidates eight to nine months
prior to the date you plan to start the business. This will give you
time to find a suitable match and give the attorney time to take
care of all preliminary start-up functions, such as assisting in the
structure of your business or helping with your business plan.

Professional Services

Legal

An attorney with broad-based expertise in business can help you
with such matters as raising capital; the legal and tax ramifications
and benefits of various business forms including sole proprietor-
ship, partnership, or corporation; name clearance to ensure that
you are not using a name already designated by another company;
legal tips on operating in your desired location; and filing any
necessary legal papers and documents for financing, establishing
your business form, and so on.

He or she will review contracts and lease agreements and can
provide support with collection problems. The lawyer you select
should also be willing and able to represent you in the event of
any claims that are brought against you or lawsuits you initiate.

Fees

Depending on your attorney's expertise, reputation, and the mar-
ket he or she serves (metropolitan area versus small town, for
example), fees will differ dramatically.

In a small community, lawyers often charge a set rate for the
job being done, while "city" lawyers typically charge by the hour
with fees ranging anywhere from $65 to $250 per hour.

This does not include the extraneous expenses involved, such
as the $300 to $1,000 cost of incorporating (depending on the
state you operate in). Neither do these fees include supplemental
costs, such as travel and telephone, incurred by the attorney in the
handling of your case.

A good way to determine the range of fees in your area is to check with your local chamber of commerce or the state bar association, generally located in the capital city. The bar association may also be able to provide you with information about a particular attorney's reputation and expertise.

When talking with potential attorneys—and when you have found one who is compatible with your needs—always be sure to ask for an outline of expenses and if he or she is willing to notify you when the fees for a particular task will be exceeded.

Accounting

The accountant you select should, early on, be able to work with you on assembling your business plan, including your projected profit and loss statements, for financing.

Down the line, as your business is being established, the accountant will help you set up your books and, once in operation, should handle your tax returns, prepare financial statements, and offer financial advice regarding tax matters, cash flow, investments to maximize the use of profits, and the tax regulations regarding employees when you are ready to hire.

Fees

As with attorneys, there is a professional association in your state capital that certifies and maintains records on the reputation and fee structures of accountants.

The basis for fee structuring does vary slightly, however, with accountants. Some charge by the hour, others by the day, and still others work on a set monthly retainer based on the estimated amount of time they will be required to spend on your work.

Be prepared, however, to pay hourly fees that average between $25 and $100, depending on the accountant's expertise and location.

Insurance

Before setting out on your search for an insurance agent, it is advisable to have already established your business form and learned exactly what insurance the law in your area requires you

to carry (fire, liability, etc.) and, if hiring employees, what kind of program you'll be offering employees, as well as your own needs for medical and life insurance.

The insurance agent you choose should be familiar with the needs of businesses and business owners, not just the standard life and disability policies. Your insurance needs will change as your business grows and expands (i.e., employee health, workers' compensation, etc.). At that point, you may want to consider key person coverage to ensure that your company can survive if a major partner or employee dies.

There are also a number of pension programs and stock-option programs available in the event you want to offer employees the incentive to increase their participation in the company in exchange for partial "ownership" down the line.

Fees

The fees for your agent's expertise are paid from your premiums, and there should be no extra charge for advice or administration of your insurance policies and programs.

Professional Services

Legal

Insurance

Accounting

11

TAXES, LICENSES, AND PERMITS

\mathbf{A}s a business owner, you are responsible for timely filing and payment of federal, state, and local taxes. Whether you have an accountant prepare your returns or you do it yourself, the task will be made much easier if you establish a systematic record-keeping system and keep your records accurate and up to date.

This includes maintaining all written documents pertaining to the financial aspect of your business: invoices, bank statements, receipts of any and all business expenses, and deposit slips.

One of the easiest ways to keep control of the "paper dragon" is to set up a 9 x 12-inch manila envelope or a file folder for each of the following categories:

♦ *Paid Bills*—both personal and business

♦ *Sales Receipts* of every product you've sold or service job you've performed

♦ *Inventory* records based on ongoing inventory control and quarterly audits

♦ *Copies of Invoices* or billing statements that are paid, with a separate file for those still due you

♦ *Receipts* for miscellaneous cash purchases

◆ *Auto/Entertainment* receipts from travel and promotional activities

All of these documents must be kept for at least five years to substantiate deductions claimed on your income tax returns in the event of an Internal Revenue Service (IRS) audit. Make up new file folders or envelopes at the beginning of each year and store the old ones in a safe place.

Preparing income tax returns is not only a time-consuming task that can take you away from the important job of running your business, but also somewhat of an art form. Tax law is a constantly changing, complicated fact of life. It is strongly recommended that you have an accountant lined up to prepare your taxes and to keep you informed of any pertinent changes during the year.

Business Deductions

The deductions that you will most likely qualify for as a business owner include operating expenses such as telephone, postage, advertising, bank service charges, travel and expense of conventions, interest, dues to professional organizations, and subscriptions to magazines pertaining to your business, among others.

Operating your business from home allows you to deduct not only a substantial portion of your rent or mortgage payment, but also percentages of your phone and utility expenses.

If you have established your business at home, you will be able to deduct that portion of the house used exclusively for business, as well as a percentage of your costs for telephone service and utilities.

Again, because of the complexity and obscurity of many of the deductions, it is best to have a professional prepare your taxes to ensure you get the full benefits to which you are entitled. Filing requirements will be determined by the type of business, the legal

structure (sole proprietorship, partnership, or corporation), income from the business, your location, state and local laws, and whether or not you have employees.

For example, as the sole proprietor of your business you would probably only be required to file personal federal and state returns based on profit or loss, with the appropriate schedules for business expenses, pay scales, self-employment and estimated taxes, and local business license fees and sales taxes.

State Income Tax

Each state has corresponding filing requirements; however, form and schedule numbers vary. Contact your state franchise tax board or your accountant for details.

Local Taxes

Taxes will vary from city to city and county to county; however, you may be required to pay city income tax and local sales tax as well as real or personal property taxes. Check with your local government offices for specifics.

Licenses and Permits

To operate your business, you will need permits and licenses based on the requirements in your area and the type of business you are operating. You will probably be required to obtain the following documents regardless of where you live.

Local Business License

Basically, this is simply a fee paid to the city or county where you are located that allows you to operate your business in that area. Some cities will also require you to pay a percentage of your gross sales every year.

Fictitious Name Statement

This is a registration for protection of your business name. Filing the fictitious name statement will also involve a city- or county-wide search to make sure you are not duplicating an existing name.

This can be done at your county hall of records. (See details in Chapter 12, "Naming Your Business.")

Seller's Permit or Resale Certificate

This is required only if you are going to be charging sales tax. Services are often exempt.

Health Permit

This is required only if you are preparing or distributing food in any manner, and involves an initial inspection and periodic follow-up inspections by health department officials.

Taxpayer Identification Number

This is available from the IRS in the case of partnerships, Subchapter S corporations, or corporations. Sole proprietors are required to have a taxpayer identification number if they pay wages to one or more employees or file pension or excise tax forms.

Your local governmental offices or your attorney will be able to give you specific licenses and permits required, as well as the corresponding fees for each as they apply to your business.

Legal Structure

As a self-employed business owner, you are required to decide on a legal form of business for tax reporting purposes. There are four basic classifications, as outlined below. If, after reviewing them, you are still unsure of which way to go, it would be advisable to talk with a lawyer about the advantages and disadvantages of each structure for your particular business.

All businesses, regardless of size, are required to maintain detailed records and file the necessary tax returns. In a corporation, regular meetings must be held. The stockholders elect a board of directors, who establish and monitor corporate policy. The board selects corporate officers to conduct the day-to-day operations of the business.

Sole proprietorships are the most convenient and least complicated form of organization for new business owners, especially

in the early stages. As your business grows, you will want to explore the options as a way of protecting your personal assets and increasing the potential for expansion capital.

Sole Proprietorship

This is the easiest to establish and is the structure many small business owners choose. A proprietorship is relatively free from government regulation, as the business has no existence apart from the owner. Profits from the operation of the business are treated as personal income for purposes of taxation, and your proprietary interest ends when you die or dissolve the business.

The major drawback of a proprietorship is that you are personally liable for any and all claims against the business and undertake the risks of the business to the extent of all assets, whether they are used in the business or personally owned. As a sole proprietor, you will be required to file self-employment tax returns and ordinarily would have to make estimated tax payments on a quarterly basis.

General Partnership

This is also an easy structure to set up and administer. Since responsibilities and capitalization are usually shared by two or more partners, taxation is based on each partner's share of business income and determined by their individual tax rates. Again, claims against the business can be filed against personal assets, and financial liability is shared equally by all partners.

Limited Partnership

This structure can be established when one or more people are willing to invest cash or tangible property in the business with active participation in the daily operations. However, there must be at least one general partner who carries unlimited financial liability and who usually maintains a full-time managerial position within the company.

The limited partners are only liable for business debts up to the amount of their investment. Although a partnership is not a taxable entity, it must figure its profit or loss and file an annual

tax return, which also becomes part of the partners' personal returns.

Corporation

In this structure, stock or shares in the business are sold to investors or stockholders, who then control the company. The advantage is that corporate stockholders are removed from any liability against personal assets. The most anyone can lose in the event of bankruptcy or a liability claim is his or her stock.

The privilege of reduced liability, however, creates paperwork (articles of incorporation and annual reports for the state tax commission and federal regulators), expenses (filing and licensing fees), and double taxation (the corporation is taxed on profits, while stockholders and elected officers are taxed individually on wages and/or dividend income).

Subchapter S Corporations

This structure has proved to be a real boon for small business owners who want the benefit of corporate protection from personal liability without double taxation. In a Subchapter S corporation, a maximum of thirty-five stockholders (who can be family members) report their share of corporate income on individual tax returns.

The corporation itself is generally exempt from federal income tax; however, it may be required to pay a tax on excess net passive investment income, capital gains, or built-in gains. To structure your company as a Subchapter S corporation, all of the shareholders must consent to the choice.

Notes

Key Points

Personal Thoughts

Additional Research

12

NAMING YOUR BUSINESS

As a pet owner, it is unlikely that you would give your German shepherd a name like Fifi. It wouldn't suit the dog's image, nor would it be appropriate. The same principle applies to choosing a name for your business.

The name you select for your business can be a tremendous asset when it defines the kind of image you want to project. You want the name to attract and appeal to potential customers, to be easily remembered over that of the competition's, and appropriate to the type of business you are starting.

Today's consumers are constantly bombarded with advertising as they go about their daily routines. Getting their attention, and holding it long enough for them to make an association between your business name and what you are offering, is imperative.

A memorable moniker can mean the difference between continued growth or a mediocre response from an audience victimized by information overload. (It is, of course, important to remember that your ultimate success depends on well-designed advertising, careful planning, and quality products and/or service.)

Naming Your Temporary Help Agency

As far as what to name the agency, most temp agency owners will advise you to be creative, to come up with something that is not too difficult to remember, and that portrays the image that you like to have associated with your business.

You might find inspiration by checking your local telephone book under temp agencies. Keep in mind that if you choose a name beginning with the letter "A," there is more likelihood of getting noticed in the Yellow Pages than if you choose a name beginning with the letter "Z." People typically start at the beginning of the listings when in the market for a service, which is why businesses are often called AA Plumbing or AAA TV Repair, for example.

If the name you select does not include your own name in the title, you must open a commercial bank account under the business name. Otherwise, checks made payable to your service could not be credited to your account, unless your bank is willing to let you sign a signature card on your personal account that covers the business as well.

If you are in a large metropolitan area, you might want to hire an attorney to conduct an investigation to check other uses of the name you select to ensure that you will not sued by any firm or large organization with the same name. If you found out that someone else has prior claim to the name you chose after you had stationery printed, ordered a sign, and opened for business, you could lose a lot of money and would be forced to redo all of your promotional efforts.

The Simple Route

Many small business owners claim their image is enhanced by the use of a straightforward name that conveys their business concept but maintains a personal sense of identity—a factor that is especially important in today's high-tech world.

Historically, in developing business names, simplicity has scored the highest points. The name you choose should be short, to the point, and easy for customers to pronounce.

As an example, when Susan Hopper made the decision to open a preschool, she grappled with names like The ABC Center,

Kiddie Land, and Now We Are Three. Finally, out of exasperation and because she felt these selections were either inappropriate or too cute, she decided to go with Susan's School, feeling it was easy to remember and conveyed exactly the personal, homey atmosphere she wanted to create. She claims that 50 percent of the parents who picked her preschool for their children from the telephone book did so because it sounded friendly and sincere.

If you do not want to name the business after yourself, you must be sure that what you do come up with is catchy enough to stand above the rest of the similar businesses in your area.

Brainstorming

Start by making a list of all the positive aspects of your business that you can think of, and call on friends and relatives to provide as many as they can come up with. Write down all the possibilities, no matter how funny or unusual they seem. A handy tool for business naming is the thesaurus, which will give you a vast number of options for commonplace names. Consider everything that springs forth from your imagination.

When you have created a list of likely candidates, get together with a group of supportive friends and family members and have a brainstorming session to either pick one of the choices you have come up with or to develop something from the ideas listed. Chances are that within a few hours, you will have a name for your business.

Catchy names are fun to design. However, make sure that it isn't so offbeat, cute, or trendy as to risk slipping into obscurity as time passes.

The Fictitious Name Statement

You are required to file a fictitious name statement with the county clerk's office. While there, you should be able to do a county-wide name check on the spot to see if there are any other businesses in the region using the name you have selected. The filing fee depends on where you live, and must be done within thirty days after you officially open your business.

It will also be necessary to publish the fictitious name in a local newspaper; the cost depends on the circulation of the paper. The county clerk's office will advise you about specific requirements in your area.

If you are starting a business that will be operating in a broader market, statewide or nationally, it is important to have your attorney do a name clearance investigation, which can take from three days to three weeks.

Your Visual Image

After you have selected a name that reflects your business image, the next step is translating it into a visual symbol or logo (logotype) to serve as the signature piece for your business. Often this involves creating a visual interpretation of your company name, but in other cases a graphic symbol or trademark is designed to serve as identification.

Some established corporate trademarks are so familiar that you can immediately identify the company even without seeing or hearing its name.

A good example of this includes the logo of the dog with his head cocked to one side. The accompanying copy reads "His Master's Voice," and it's a good bet that you recognize this as the logo for RCA. Another effective logo is the avant-garde apple that identifies Apple computer products.

If you do not have the graphic skills necessary to design a logo with impact, get in touch with your nearest art association (listed in the phone book or available through local art supply shops or galleries) or call a nearby college or university. Ask the head of the art department if your design can be given as a class assignment or if he or she could recommend a student to do the job for a small fee. It will give students practical application, and the design can be used later in their portfolio. You can offer cash or a prize for the best design. The students will undoubtedly meet the challenge with enthusiasm and give you a number of good samples and ideas from which to choose.

Selecting a Typeface

Save sample logos and advertisements that use a typeface you like. Type is an extremely important element of logo design and can also pinpoint the precise image you hope to express. Type not only presents the basic message, it can play a powerful role in the overall appearance of your logo and can actually create atmosphere. A chart of some of the more popular typefaces is included at the end of this chapter.

When deciding on a typeface for your logo, visit print shops or typesetting studios and look at their typeface books. They offer both the usual, functional varieties as well as a selection of unique typefaces that can really dress up your logo and subtly portray a specific personality such as dignified, fun, powerful, classic, or cutting edge.

Have the logo and your business information (address, phone number, etc.) set in more than the one typeface so that you can see how they will look when printed. Also ask to have them set in both small (10-point to 12-point for business cards) and larger (20- to 24-point for letterhead) versions. Once typeset, you will be able to make a final decision about which typeface suits the image you want to project.

Historically, in developing business names, simplicity has scored the highest points. The name you choose should be short, to the point, and easy for consumers to pronounce.

Typesetters generally have a minimum fee based on the amount of time they spend on a job, which can vary from $15 per hour in a small city to $50 per hour in a business area, as high as $100 per hour in major metropolitan areas. That's why it's important to shop around.

Word processing specialists or independent desktop publishers can also provide a variety of typefaces and formats at less expense. Since you will only be having a few words typeset, the

time and cost required to set them in several different styles should certainly be affordable.

Business Cards and Stationery

The typeface and logo you eventually choose will be used on your letterhead; in your display and telephone advertising; on all promotional materials, including flyers, brochures, and announcements; on your sign; and on statements and invoices.

They will also be used on your business cards, one of the most inexpensive and convenient ways to inform people about your service or product. Once you have had cards printed, be generous. Give one to everyone you meet and always be sure to carry a supply wherever you go.

Most fast-print copy centers are prepared to help you if you decide not to design your own business cards and stationery. They have samples of business forms, letterheads, and cards with various styles to choose from. Make sure that your company name, logo, address, and phone number are included where necessary. If you have a fax and/or toll-free number, be sure those numbers are included. When someone looks at your card or letterhead, it must tell them instantly who you are, what your business is, and how you can be reached.

Sample Typefaces

Helvetica
ABCDEFGHIJ
abcdefghij

Helvetica Black
ABCDEFGHIJ
abcdefghij

Helvetica Condensed
ABCDEFGHIJ
abcdefghij

ITC Eras
ABCDEFGHIJ
abcdefghij

ITC Eras Demi
ABCDEFGHIJ
abcdefghij

ITC Eras Bold
ABCDEFGHIJ
abcdefghij

Korinna
ABCDEFGHIJ
abcdefghij

Korinna Bold
ABCDEFGHIJ
abcdefghij

Rose Round
ABCDEFGHIJ
abcdefghij

Lubalin Graph
ABCDEFGHIJ
abcdefghij

Britannic Light
ABCDEFGHIJ
abcdefghij

Britannic Bold
ABCDEFGHIJ
abcdefghij

Brush Script
ABCDEFGHIJ
abcdefghij

Optima
ABCDEFGHIJ
abcdefghij

Optima Italic
ABCDEFGHIJ
abcdefghij

Optima Bold
ABCDEFGHIJ
abcdefghij

Park Avenue
ABCDEFGHIJ
abcdefghij

Palatino
ABCDEFGHIJ
abcdefghij

Palatino Italic
ABCDEFGHIJ
abcdefghij

Palatino Bold
ABCDEFGHIJ
abcdefghij

Garamond Book
ABCDEFGHIJ
abcdefghij

Garamond Ultra
ABCDEFGHIJ
abcdefghij

Times Roman
ABCDEFGHIJ
abcdefghij

Times Italic
ABCDEFGHIJ
abcdefghij

ITC Fenice Regular
ABCDEFGHIJ
abcdefghij

ITC Fenice Bold
ABCDEFGHIJ
abcdefghij

ITC Fenice Ultra
ABCDEFGHIJ
abcdefghij

Eurostile
ABCDEFGHIJ
abcdefghij

Eurostile Bold
ABCDEFGHIJ
abcdefghij

Eurostile Extended
ABCDEFGHIJ
abcdefghij

Notes

Key Points

Personal Thoughts

Additional Research

13

DEVELOPING A BUSINESS PLAN

Developing your business plan is the most important process you will undertake in your career as an entrepreneur, regardless of the size or type of business you have decided to start.

A well-thought-out business plan will serve as a blueprint while your idea turns into a recognizable entity and as it grows into a stable and profitable venture. Too often we hear former small business owners say they probably could have made a success of their business if they had only known what to expect from the beginning...and that is where the business plan comes in.

Unfortunately, too many new entrepreneurs are unfamiliar with the importance of planning, or consider themselves an exception and feel they can succeed by winging it or dealing with problems as they arise. Not true!

Every business, whether a large commercial venture or a small home-based enterprise, needs to analyze its potential, examine its strengths and weaknesses, and determine the future of the organization. It works for the major corporations and it will work for you, especially once you become involved in the day-to-day operations of the business. Having a business plan will give you the freedom to follow the steps you have carefully laid out with regard to budgeting, the success ratio of your product or service, the hiring of employees, and other growth decisions.

Advantages of the Business Plan

Once you have made the decision to become a business owner, you must devise a specific statement that clearly outlines *what* you plan to do, *when* you plan to do it, and *how* you will accomplish the short- and long-term goals.

Not only will this keep you on track, it will serve as an indicator to others of your sincerity and knowledge when you go out to find start-up or expansion capital, and it will serve as the foundation of your financing proposal.

The other advantage is that the actual task of putting your business plan together will help you define and clarify every step of your concept and, if done in a conscientious and objective manner, will point out potential trouble spots that can be addressed before they become major problems.

If all the necessary components are covered, it will put your business on the road to profit. It is a sure bet that, down the road, if you find your business is not generating the income you had originally projected, this is because you didn't include one or more of the basic business plan requirements.

Not a Guessing Game

Like any other major project, preparing a business plan involves time and research. It shouldn't be a guessing game. It will be necessary to ask yourself some very specific questions and to answer them thoughtfully and honestly. The business plan is your foundation, so build it carefully to ensure that it works at optimum efficiency for your needs. And make sure it is typed, orderly, and good looking so that you and others can recognize its importance in the professional scheme of your expanding operation.

An important aspect to remember is that your business plan is not cast in stone. In fact, what makes a business plan so great is that it invites revisions as your business changes and grows. This makes it a companion in your success and, by reviewing it regularly, a partner in your progress.

The best way to approach your business plan is to take paper and pen and devote a few hours to coming up with some hard answers. Of course, you will want to condense your answers to fit

into specific segments within the plan, including (in order of appearance) Concept and Feasibility, Legal Structure, Product or Service, Customer Base, Marketing and Production Goals, Personnel (your résumé and Entrepreneurial Profile and those of any other key personnel), and Financial Statements.

It is advisable to start each segment on a separate page and to create a table of contents to place in the front. Be sure it is well-written and organized, neatly typed, and bound in a report folder to preserve it and give it a professional look, especially when using it as a sales tool to convince lenders.

Key Questions to Ask Yourself

The first question you must ask yourself is: "Why am I interested in this particular business?" Probably the answer will be something to the effect of wanting to be your own boss and making money...independence and income.

This answer is fine as a personal goal, but it isn't going to be good enough if you are planning to approach potential lenders for funding. They will want to see an overview of your business concept, why you are convinced it will be successful, and where it fits in the scheme of similar businesses in your town or city.

The next question you must ask is: "What is my product or service?" This may seem like a ridiculous question since you know your product is gift baskets or your service is catering, local sightseeing tours, or whatever, but it goes deeper. Your written response will include details about the service or a description of your product (preferably positive), with a focus on why customers will be inclined to work with you.

Additional questions to consider should include

- ♦ Why do I believe there is a need for my product or service?
- ♦ How do I plan to develop my business over the next five years?
- ♦ How much will I charge to ensure value to the customer and profit for myself?
- ♦ Who are my suppliers?

◆ Who are my customers?

◆ What equipment do I need to start the business?

◆ How much inventory and supplies do I need for start-up?

◆ What will it cost?

◆ Who is my competition and where is it located?

◆ What does the competition offer and how will I offer something different to attract customers?

◆ What changes are occurring in my marketing area that will impact my business in the future?

◆ What are my estimated sales figures for each of the next five years? (A guesstimate can be based on researching similar businesses in the area.)

◆ How will I advertise and promote my business and how will I pay for it?

◆ How and where is my product going to be manufactured?

◆ What is involved in the production—materials, labor, costs?

◆ Where will my service be performed?

◆ What equipment is required for my service and what are the costs for leasing versus purchasing?

◆ What are other overhead expenses (rent, employees, etc.)?

◆ How many people will be involved in the business and what are their qualifications?

◆ If I don't have employees, am I qualified to run the business myself?

By talking with people in similar businesses, as well as suppliers and direct competitors, and your local chamber of commerce, you will gather a great deal of information, both positive and negative, about your potential business. People love to talk about their success and, if you ask in the right way, their failures.

If you operate like an investigative reporter for a few days while doing research for your business plan, it's guaranteed that

you will obtain plenty of good, solid information. A Service Corps of Retired Executives (SCORE) representative through the Small Business Administration can also provide assistance or tell you about resources that can help you develop a realistic business plan.

Trade associations, listed in reference books available at your local library, can provide you with invaluable details on industry facts and figures, such as the percentage of gross sales that should be spent on advertising, the percentage that is typically paid for rent in your particular business, and how to price your product or service.

The final item to include in this section of your business plan, when and if presenting it for financing, is a personal résumé, designed to emphasize your general business management experience and your expertise within your specific area.

Describe the job duties for every job you have held, including any special aspects that pertain directly to the business.

If you cannot prepare the résumé, it is worth the minor fee to have it done professionally. The results will pay for the cost hundreds of times over.

Show me a person with an obsession about succeeding and a solid business plan, and I'll show you a good risk.
Anonymous Loan Officer

Financial Statements

Once you have written your overview and description sheets, it's time to get down to numbers. This is the key to your business plan and, unfortunately, the area where many entrepreneurs get bogged down. But without an understanding about the numbers involved, you can never expect to be a good manager and really shouldn't be surprised if you run into money problems within the first year.

Again, utilizing the resources indicated above—chamber of commerce, trade associations—you will need to work up your financial pages to include the following components, which most lenders will want to see projected for one and five years.

◆ *Projected operating expenses.* This projected number includes materials, advertising, salaries for employees or outside labor, and other expenses directly related to the cost of doing business.

◆ *Estimate of gross (before tax) sales revenue.* If the business is not yet operating, base your estimate on research figures from trade associations and what the local market dictates. If business is underway, base your estimate on how many items or hours of service you plan to sell and the average price you plan to charge.

◆ *How you arrived at the figures for these statements.* Generally, you would base your figures on assumptions made about the number of months of operation, estimated number of sales, and the average amount versus the cost of each sale.

◆ *Cost of equipment and furnishings.* Get estimated quotes, whether you are planning to purchase or lease these items.

◆ *Cost of materials.* You need to know how much items will cost for production, if applicable, and for maintenance on equipment needed to run the business.

◆ *Additional operating expenses.* You should research prices for rent, telephone and other utilities, business taxes and license fees, office supplies, and even decorating costs. Include a category called "other" to provide a cushion for unexpected expenses.

◆ *Balance sheet.* This shows assets, such as equipment and operating capital you already have, and liabilities or debts and expenses. If the business has not yet started, this would be a personal balance sheet indicating your net worth, listing all possessions of any value plus cash, stock, and other holdings, minus financial responsibilities.

◆ *Leasehold improvements.* If you are planning to rent a commercial location or redesign a room within your home strictly for business, estimate cleaning and restoration costs in this statement.

By investing the time and energy into this portion of the business plan, you will absorb the numbers into your consciousness and be able to recognize, at a glance, when your costs exceed your profit margin or when you are in a position to start expanding.

If money matters are absolutely beyond your comprehension at this point, it would pay to hire someone to work with you to develop the financial pages of the plan. There are business consultants and accountants who will probably charge you a substantial amount, or you can approach the accounting or business department of the nearest college and see if there is a qualified student available to help you.

No matter who you find to assist you, however, be sure to stay involved in the process...the discipline and hard work will guarantee success.

Notes

Key Points

Personal Thoughts

Additional Research

14

FINANCING YOUR BUSINESS

Starting your business without having sufficient capital is setting yourself up for problems from the beginning. Undercapitalization is cited as one of the major reasons why businesses do not succeed; however, this simply boils down to bad planning.

If you research and record all the goals, marketing data, equipment and supply requirements, and financial needs of your venture before actually opening your doors, you will be able to see at a glance how much you need to get going, and *why you need it.* That way, there will be no surprises and no reason that your business should suffer from lack of capitalization.

It is important to have the financial resources to cover all your preliminary planning and start-up costs, including expenses incurred to research the feasibility of your business and expenses required to set up shop, from equipment and supplies to advertising and utility setup charges. In addition, you need a surplus to carry you over personally until the business becomes productive. The Cash Flow Statement, Start-up Costs Worksheet, and Projected Expense Statement forms provided in Chapter 8 will help you determine these expenses.

If, after developing your business plan, you find that your personal resources are not enough to open the business, there are other options available.

The four most common methods include

◆ Starting the business on a part-time basis while holding a full-time job to cover expenses

◆ Taking on a limited partner

◆ Going to friends or family members for the money you need

◆ Applying for a loan through a commercial lender or the Small Business Administration (SBA)

There are, of course, pros and cons to each of these options.

Starting Out Part-time

Starting your business on a part-time or "moonlighting" basis is a decision that must be made based on the nature of the business. If you are planning to capitalize on your skills in upholstering, for example, you should have no trouble building up the business at night and on weekends.

It is perfectly feasible to start small, using your garage or a spare room as your production facility and purchasing an answering machine for potential customers to leave a message while you are at your regular job. When you get home, you simply call them back to discuss prices and arrange a time when it is convenient to pick up the piece of furniture to be upholstered.

On the other hand, if you are planning to start a temporary help agency, it would be in your best interest to go into it on a full-time, dedicated basis, as your potential customers will want fast results and will call someone else if they are even slightly discouraged. A recorded message, for example, is likely to put them off.

Moonlighting will work with some businesses, but before exploring it as an option you must determine if your limited availability will affect your credibility, if you really have the time and energy to work at a regular job while trying to build a business (not to mention keeping up with family responsibilities), and whether your ultimate goal is to be self-employed or just to earn a few extra dollars.

Considering a Partner

A limited partner is one who will put up the money you need and step into the background to let you run the business the way you see fit. You must be sure, however, to have your attorney draw up a precise partnership agreement that covers every eventuality. Partnerships are typically entered into with the best intentions and the unwavering belief that the business will be successful.

Since this is not always the case—and even if it were—it is a businesslike move to ensure that such aspects as decision making, distribution of profits and losses, contributions of partners, and handling disputes and changes are outlined and approved by all the partners.

Approaching a Lender

Once you have your business plan and other paperwork prepared, decide which lending association you want to approach. Certainly, if you have a stable record with a checking or savings account at your regular bank or savings and loan, that is the place to try first. Set up an appointment with the bank manager or loan officer to make your request and explain why you feel your business venture is worth the bank's investment.

Be aware, however, that banks are more likely to provide you with a loan payable within five or ten years, as opposed to savings and loans, which are more interested in long-term loans, such as for mortgages. Credit unions operate in a similar manner to banks; however, you generally have to be a member. If you do belong to a credit union it could be your best bet, as it offers lower interest rates and can be more flexible in lending decisions.

If you do not want to run a loan through your bank, consider talking with other local small business owners. Very often, they can steer you to a regional, often independently owned bank or savings and loan that is empathetic to and supportive of new businesses. In that case, proceed as mentioned earlier and arrange a meeting with the manager or loan officer.

Present your case in a friendly yet professional manner. Be realistic and honest about your needs. Do not underbid because you worry that you will not get a loan if you ask for too much. It

is always better to start with a higher figure than you actually need so you have a strong negotiating edge.

In addition, most lenders have a pretty good idea about start-up and operating costs of new businesses and are much less likely to give you, and risk losing, a small loan for a business they know calls for more capital. They will be more willing to work with you if you are realistic and knowledgeable about your needs.

If, after your first try, the answer is no, ask for reasons why you are being turned down so you can restructure your presentation. Turn rejection into a learning tool to redefine and polish your material and to develop new negotiating strategies. There are always other lenders you can approach, and the law of averages dictates that you will get your loan if the idea is solid and it is apparent that you have researched the feasibility of starting a business in your particular area.

Money brings some happiness. But, after a certain point, it just brings more money.

Neil Simon

Financing Methods

"Friendly Financing"

The third option, raising capital through friends or family members, is probably one of the methods most often used. The advantage of getting a loan from a personal contact is that he or she knows you, undoubtedly trusts your ability to make the business go, and won't require much in the way of substantiating paperwork, such as complex loan applications, financial statements, etc. In addition, you will most likely be able to negotiate a very low interest rate on the loan.

The major disadvantage, according to entrepreneurs who have taken this route, is if the friendly lender decides that he or she wants to provide input on the care and maintenance of your business. This problem, however, can be eliminated by a thorough

business discussion prior to accepting the loan. In other words, choose your investor carefully!

The second problem has to do with repayment of the loan. Even though you have a loose agreement in writing with your lender, because of friendship or family ties there may come a point when Uncle Bill needs that $10,000 *tomorrow* to take care of a personal obligation. You can't possibly come up with the money overnight, Uncle Bill gets angry, and that whole side of the family turns against you.

The flip side of the coin is if the business fails and you are unable to pay Uncle Bill the $10,000 he put up. There are any number of unpleasant situations, so you must be sure in the beginning to think about the importance of the relationship you have with the potential lender, how the best and the worst of circumstances would affect your relationship, and whether you then could justify asking for money.

Commercial Lenders

If you are not able to, or if you decide against approaching friends or relatives for financial assistance, the next step is a bank, a savings and loan, or a credit union. Before approaching any of these commercial lenders, you must have carefully developed your business plan, which will include the following documents.

1. A résumé or statement outlining your background and capability to operate the business, plus a similar statement about any key employees or partners in the business.

2. A statement of business and personal goals.

3. A description of the business, including market research for your product or service.

4. Details on how the business is going to be structured (sole proprietorship, partnership, corporation).

5. A projection of profit and loss for a minimum of one year (five years is preferable), which means you will have investigated how similar businesses are doing.

6. An outline of how much money you need—and why—to keep the business solvent and to support yourself and your family for at least a year.

In addition, you will be required to provide a personal balance sheet that lists your assets (real estate, a car, valuable personal property) and liabilities (mortgage payments, credit card debts) along with a credit application that outlines your personal financial history, so a determination can be made on your ability to pay back the loan. The lender will follow through by requesting a credit report from an independent agency to help with the decision.

The main point to remember when applying for a loan with a commercial institution is that lenders aren't as concerned about the amount loaned as they are about how and when they are going to get the money back!

Paying Back the Loan

When you apply for financing, the burden of proof as it relates to repayment rests with you. No one would knowingly grant a loan to an individual or a business that he or she had doubts about. As a borrower, your responsibility is to show that you will be able to pay back the loan according to the terms agreed to by you and the lender. If you have a good credit history, a credit report will indicate as much.

The Small Business Administration

The Small Business Administration (SBA) often goes where no other lender will tread and, as such, is a lender of last resort. The SBA is a government agency that is well known for providing financing to entrepreneurs who have been repeatedly turned down by commercial lenders, which, in fact, you generally must be before the SBA will consider backing you.

After your loan request with a commercial institution has been denied, you can file an application with the nearest branch of the SBA. It is a good idea to make an appointment with a Service Corps of Retired Executives (SCORE) representative (a man or woman who volunteers his or her time to the SBA-SCORE program to advise new and established business owners). Your SCORE

representative will lead you through the complex paperwork required by the SBA before it makes a decision.

In addition, SCORE volunteers are usually straightforward, knowledgeable men and women who will walk through your business plans with you and offer constructive suggestions. Once the paperwork is completed, a commercial lender will make the loan under the SBA Lender Certification Program, knowing that the government is willing to insure it.

We recommend this option only after you have been turned down by three or more banks, because of the time factor involved in gaining approval and also because of the extensive follow-up reports required by the SBA. It is, however, a viable option and one that has helped thousands of dedicated entrepreneurs realize their goals.

Venture Capitalists

Money is available to businesses that are already established and seeking working or expansion capital from groups of investors known as venture capitalists. These groups can vary from a few local businesspeople with money to invest to major investment companies that are connected with large corporations or financial organizations.

Venture capital is not like a straightforward business loan. It is usually dependent on a minimum $100,000 investment and, therefore, is not suited to every business situation. Typically, venture capitalists are interested in companies that have a track record, a proven position in the market, and a solid growth projection.

But, like a bank or other lending association, venture capitalists want to see a written business plan and a prospectus of future projections. They are looking at your background, the market, the kind of funding you want, and your past financial record.

Since venture capitalists are looking to earn from 10 to 15 percent on their investment over a relatively short period, they will want to spend a great deal of time talking with you and your associates, customers, and suppliers.

Before considering venture capital, we advise discussing it carefully with an attorney who can help you investigate different

groups to figure out the best investment structure, and who can work with the group's attorney on drawing up an agreement that protects you. Many venture capitalists will want to own part of your company.

This is an option to be considered only when your company is well established and undergoing rapid growth pains and should be approached with great understanding of the situation.

Other Financing Options

Loan Companies

Loan companies are good sources of funding. However, interest rates are high, and they will generally want to have substantial collateral, such as the equity in your house, on record before making a loan.

Insurance Companies

Your insurance carrier may be willing to make an investment in your small business, using your insurance policy as collateral, or you may even have enough cash value in your policy, depending on the face amount, to provide substantial start-up capital. If this is the case, you will only be required to pay quarterly or semiannual interest payments on the cash value you have taken out.

Factoring

In this instance, a factoring company "buys" your accounts receivable and advances you a percentage of the full amount due. This is a viable option for well-established service companies that work on a billing basis.

Cosigner

If you have a relative or friend who is already an established business owner or, at least, a homeowner with a solid credit rating, it might be worth your while to ask if he or she would cosign on a loan application with you. Although you are still responsible for repayment of the loan, the bank is assured that, in the event you default for any reason, the cosigner will guarantee the obligation.

It is sometimes difficult to find someone who will do this, but again it doesn't hurt to ask, especially if it is a last resort.

Starting Small

Even if you know your particular business is valid and that you have the ability to make it succeed, be certain that your business plan is realistic. If you have chosen to start a business on a grand scale but have minimal capital and little business experience, it may be best to begin a smaller, less elaborate operation at first.

You'll require less "seed money" and will be in a low-risk position while learning the operations of a business and seeing if you can handle all the variables of business ownership while making it grow.

Smaller businesses have proven to be a great way to learn successful methods, as well as a vehicle for ironing out the many small, often overlooked, details. The profits you gain from a smaller venture can be used to expand or invest in bigger business ideas. And an added bonus is that when you are ready to approach investors or lending institutions, you will be able to show them that you already have a solid track record and a working knowledge of business procedures.

*The journey of a thousand miles
begins with a single step.*

Chinese Proverb

What to Do When Asking for Money

1. ***Be sure to ask.*** This may seem like a gross statement of the obvious, but you would be amazed at the number of small business owners we've heard about who never ask because they are afraid of being turned down.

 Unless you are independently wealthy and pursuing your business as a humanitarian effort, it is unlikely that you are in a position to run your business and earn enough money to support you, your family, and the

operation—especially during the first year. Remember the old adage: It *takes* money to *make* money.

If you run a low-budget business, you will probably get a low-budget response. If you are determined to make it work, be sure you have sufficient capital to make it work the right way.

Fear is often a factor: "I don't want to ask, in case I'm told no." Well, that's the worst thing that can happen. But if you persevere and are serious about your venture, someone will inevitably say yes!

And don't overlook friends and family; they can be your most ardent supporters if you have given them reason in the past to believe you are responsible and determined to succeed.

2. ***Know how much you need.*** Lenders are familiar with the financial demands of business operation and will respect your request if you have obviously done your homework and can talk intelligently about your needs.

3. ***Be direct and confident.*** If you believe in your business and in your ability to make it work, others will be convinced as well. Never apologize for mistakes you feel you have made in the past.

Simply present the facts honestly, even if it includes revealing an error in judgment you have made somewhere along the line, and assure the lender that he or she will be making a smart decision by investing in you.

4. ***Think positively.*** If you need $50,000, ask for $50,000. Never underestimate the potential to provide. Remember: It is easier to negotiate and deal with one lender for a single amount than it is to keep paperwork and relationships strong with several, all of whom have contributed to the pot.

5. ***Ask again.*** If they trusted you once and you have lived up to the stipulations of the contract, ask again—that goes for commercial lending institutions as well as friends and relatives. When it comes to borrowing money, a proven record is what it's all about, and if you have established

yours, keep it active. It will be your passport to profit when the chips are down.

6. ***Know when to borrow.*** If you have worked out your business plan and know you can survive while getting the business off the ground, start exploring your financing options ahead of time. Don't wait until the last minute when you will be forced to act and will have to take a less-than-favorable opportunity. The same theory applies if your business is already established. By examining your financial position on a regular basis, you will be able to project how much you will need at a given point for expansion purposes. Always be aware.

7. ***Don't borrow if it is not necessary.*** Many businesses can be started for under $1,000. This is called "starting on a shoestring" and can be done with a variety of businesses. Services, for example, often rely strictly on the owner's knowledge and expertise and can be set up quickly and inexpensively.

 If this is the case with the business you have in mind, then try to avoid borrowing money, which can be an expensive and timely proposition.

Establishing Credit

Is it possible to get a loan even if you have never established credit? Yes, it is. If you prefer to pay cash rather than incur high interest charges on loans or credit cards, you can still qualify for a loan based on personal assets or by having a friend or relative with a good credit rating cosign for you on the loan. This puts the obligation on the cosigner, so be sure the terms of the loan are clearly spelled out in a written agreement to the satisfaction of everyone involved.

But, if your personal assets are minimal and you cannot find a cosigner, your best bet is to put off starting the business for four to six months while you establish credit. The best place to start is with a major department store. A store will issue you a credit card based on a very simple examination of your income and employment history. When you receive the card, charge about $100 worth

of merchandise and pay it off according to the schedule provided. Within a few months, you will have proven yourself to be credit-worthy, which will greatly improve your chances of getting a loan from a lending institution.

Another way to establish credit—and credibility—is to open a checking account at the bank you have decided to approach for a loan. Banks generally require a minimum deposit of between $50 and $100. Make it a point to meet the branch manager and/or the loan officer and establish an ongoing relationship with them by stopping by to say hello when you are in the bank.

Within a few months, apply for a small personal loan, working with your new acquaintance, of course. Make your payments according to the prearranged schedule. Then when you are ready to request a more substantial amount of money to cover your start-up expenses, you will be recognized as a customer with a loan history at that institution.

Notes

Key Points

Personal Thoughts

Additional Research

15

Record Keeping:
Your Business Lifeline

The motivating factor in any business is profit, which can be explained as the money left over after all the bills—everything from supplies to rent to salaries to taxes—are paid.

Building a profitable business is not something that can be left to chance; it must be planned, and a systematic method of record keeping must be developed to help you monitor income and expenses.

You should expect that during the early days of your business, your profits are going to be minimal as you become established. But it is possible, with even simple record-keeping procedures, to prepare yourself for lean periods and control day-to-day expenses to ensure that you are, at least, breaking even. In addition, financial records are required for tax purposes, and dealing with them systematically can help you avoid an incredibly overwhelming task at tax time.

Record Keeping Can Be Simple

Some people cringe at the thought of record keeping or feel it is a waste of valuable time. Usually, these attitudes are based on a lack

of knowledge and the feeling that it is a difficult job. There is, however, no other way to analyze your cash flow and make sure you are pricing products or services high enough to realize a profit.

In truth, record keeping is not a complicated process. If you have ever balanced a checkbook or planned a household budget, you have performed several of the same steps that are necessary for implementing a bookkeeping system for your business. And the good news is that keeping business records does not have to be either complicated or time consuming.

We know of entrepreneurs who opt for total simplicity by using the "shoebox" method—every sales record, receipt for expenses, and bank statement gets tossed into a box. This system has two distinct drawbacks. One may not become apparent until tax time, when you attempt to wade through and organize each sheet of paper to prepare your tax return. The other, more critical drawback is that it is virtually impossible to maintain an accurate picture of your financial situation when you stockpile, rather than record, business transactions.

In order to understand your cash flow, it is important to be able to see monies earned, monies paid out, current balances, and outstanding debts.

In fact, you should be able to answer the following questions with just a quick review of your records.

- ◆ What was my income last year (week, month)?
- ◆ What were my expenses?
- ◆ How do income and expenses compare with last year (week, month)?
- ◆ What was my profit (loss) last year (week, month)?
- ◆ Where can I cut back on expenses?
- ◆ Who and how much do I currently owe on outstanding debts?
- ◆ Who owes me money and how much?
- ◆ What are my assets, liabilities, and net worth?
- ◆ Is my inventory in line with demand?

♦ How much cash do I have available? How much credit?

♦ Am I able to pay myself this month (week)?

♦ Are my figures in line with projected financial goals?

The records you need to be able to answer most of these questions are your cash journal, a balance sheet, and a bank reconciliation. A simple single-entry system, as indicated later in this chapter, where you can record disbursements (cash paid out) and receipts (cash taken in) will form the base of your record-keeping system.

If you can organize your kitchen,
you can organize your life.

Dr. Louis Parrish

Double-Entry Bookkeeping

You may want to consider a double-entry system, which involves recording each transaction twice; once as a debit (simply the left column of the ledger) and once as a credit (the right column of the ledger). For example, if you were to sell a product for $100, the transactions recorded in a double-entry system would be as follows: The $100 would be written as a *credit* in your sales account, since merchandise is going out of the business, and $100 would be recorded as a *debit* in your cash account since money was coming into the business.

This is a complex and time-consuming process that is often best left to an accountant, who will need the information to create a monthly trial balance and other financial statements, including your year-end tax reports.

Bookkeeping Debits and Credits

Debits

- ◆ Cash receipts
- ◆ Purchases
- ◆ Expenses, such as rent and wages

Credits

- ◆ Cash payments
- ◆ Sales of services or merchandise
- ◆ Earnings, including interest

Single-Entry Bookkeeping

You can, however, set up a simple single-entry system, which will tie in directly with your accountant's requirements, or check out the standardized bookkeeping systems available at office supply or stationery stores. The stores will provide all the necessary forms and documents in a bound book.

A system should contain forms for recording monthly income and expenses, summary sheets from which you can create a balance sheet, and listings of legal deductions for income tax reporting. In addition, the trade association for your field should be able to provide you with systems developed exclusively for use in the industry, which you can use or adapt according to the specific circumstances of your business.

The final method is to purchase a cash journal and set up your own monthly system. (We've used Office Assistance, a small secretarial service that has been in operation for one month, as an example.) Any of the above-mentioned methods are acceptable, as long as you understand the entry process and can read the results.

Make Record Keeping a Daily Task

Short of paying someone else, the easiest way to be sure your records are kept up to date is to incorporate the task into your daily

or weekly routine. Many small business owners make it a habit to enter their sales, expenses, and other financial information at the end of each working day. It keeps them continually aware of their financial situation and ensures that there will never be any cash-flow surprises.

The process shouldn't take more than fifteen minutes for normal transactions, and it will save hours of pencil pushing and frustration down the line. What's important is that you'll always know where you stand financially.

Setting Up the Books

Now, using Office Assistance, we will examine the various elements required for basic record-keeping duties.

Office Assistance has been in business for one month. Two months ago, Bill Miller, president of Office Assistance, opened a new business bank account with $10,000.00, his start-up capital from a personal savings account.

At the same time, he rented a small office in a downtown building for $350.00 a month, but had to pay the first month's rent, and a deposit of the last month's rent, for a total outlay of $700.00.

His fictitious name statement, which he got approved through the local county clerk's office, cost $10.00, and publishing it in a regional newspaper cost $45.00.

The initial month's lease and a deposit on a computer cost him $275.00, plus $50.00 for a maintenance agreement. However, he will own the $2,000.00 computer when his payment schedule is completed.

He found a brand-new calculator at a garage sale for $25.00 and is going to use a desk, table, lamp, and chairs from home (value $350.00) to decorate the office. Phone-line installation was $150.00, and he purchased a two-line telephone for $79.50.

An artist friend designed his logo and letterhead on a computer for only $25.00 and a $6.95 lunch. He had his stationery ($35.00), business cards ($60.00), and brochures ($23.50) produced through a local copy shop for a total of $118.50.

A 2 × 2-inch display ad in the local newspaper will cost him $370.00 for a week, and he is planning to mail 100 of his brochures to local businesses selected from the phone book. Stamps will cost $29.00 for the mailing. Office supplies, including typing paper, staples, paper clips, etc., set him back $45.00. A journal for record keeping cost $7.95 and a packet of invoices $5.95, for a grand total of $58.90.

Since he doesn't know how to type, Bill hired his niece to work 20 hours a week for $10.00 per hour on an independent contractor basis so he doesn't have to pay social security or unemployment taxes.

During the first month, he has billed and been paid $700.00. However, he has two clients who still owe him a total of $400.00. Bill dutifully records information in his cash journal at the end of each working day. He uses source documents, including his check-book register, receipts from cash purchases, and billing invoices as the basis for his entries. The following cash journal illustrations are for May (prior to opening the doors of his business) and June (his first actual month in business).

Bill's expenses for May and June were $3,108.75. Of course, part of that is for start-up expenses, such as deposits on his rent and computer, installation costs, and one-time fictitious name filing and publishing. His income for the first month was $700.00.

Office Assistance
Cash Journal for May

Date	Check or Invoice #	Detail	(Debit) Expense	(Credit) Income
5/1	100	Rawlins Real Estate (rent & dep)	$700.00	
5/5	101	County Clerk (fictitious name)	10.00	
5/7	102	The Herald (publishing FNS)	45.00	
5/9	103	Ed's Keyboards (IBM l-mo. & dep)	275.00	
5/9	104	Ed's Keyboards (maint. agreement)	50.00	
5/12	105	Mary Smith (calculator purchase)	25.00	
5/18	106	Telephone Co. (line installation)	150.00	
5/20	107	Phone Store (2-line phone)	79.50	
5/22	108	Ray Brown (logo design)	25.00	
5/24	Cash	The Hungry Dog (lunch/Ray Brown)	6.95	
5/28	109	The Copy Spot (brochures, cards)	118.50	
5/29	110	The Herald (advertising)	370.00	
		Total Expense & Income (May)	**$1,854.95**	**$00.00**

Office Assistance
Cash Journal for June

Date	Check or Invoice #	Detail	(Debit) Expense	(Credit) Income
6/4	111	U.S.P.O. (stamps for mailing)	$29.00	
6/6	112	Office Stationers (supplies, invoices, etc.)	58.90	
6/7	A1	W. Smith		$62.50
6/8	A2	Art Association		112.50
6/9	A3	T. Williams		22.00
6/9	113	Judy Miller (typing fee)	200.00	
6/10	A4	Bank of Cutterville		75.00
6/10	A5	WKTR-FM		120.50
6/13	A6	J. Johnson		43.50
6/15	114	Rawlins Real Estate (rent)	350.00	
6/15	A7	C. Lewis		73.50
6/15	A8	R. Swell		90.00
6/16	115	Judy Miller (typing fee)	200.00	
6/19	A9	W. Smith		52.50
6/23	116	Judy Miller (typing fee)	200.00	
6/26	117	Phone company (bill)	15.90	
6/27	A10	K. Black		48.00
6/30	118	Judy Miller (typing fee)	200.00	
		Total Expense & Income (June)	**$1,253.80**	**$700.00**

By deducting his expenses from his income, he can see that, at the moment, his business is showing a loss of $2,408.75.

Although Bill has only been in business for a month, he is curious about his company's financial worth and decides to work up a balance sheet to get the answer. The calculation, as indicated in the example, is the amount owned (assets) minus the amount due to creditors (liabilities), which equals his worth.

Balance Sheet (as of June 30)

Assets		Liabilities	
Cash on hand & in bank	$6,191.25	Ed's Keyboards	$1,725.00
(Capital balance &		*(Balance on IBM)*	
June income)		Unpaid rent *(July)*	350.00
Office equipment	2,000.00	Taxes *(estimated)*	75.00
(Includes full value			
of IBM even though			
not paid off)			
Office furniture	350.00	**Liabilities**	**$2,150.00**
Accounts receivable			
(outstanding invoices			
for work already done)	400.00		
Total Assets	**$8,941.25**	**CAPITAL**	**$6,791.25**
		Total Liabilities	**$8,941.25**

The figure Bill is most interested in is the CAPITAL amount in the Liabilities column. This is the amount remaining after what Bill owes is subtracted from his current assets and is what his business is worth at the end of June. In other words, if he decided to try to sell his business right now, he could realistically ask that amount as a selling price. Of course, Bill probably wouldn't get that amount because he has not yet become established enough to warrant someone buying the business, unless he or she was looking for a "turnkey" operation—in other words, a business to just walk into and get going immediately.

This information is valuable when Bill goes to apply for expansion capital or for credit on future purchases he plans to

make. His balance sheet will change each time he prepares it (probably quarterly in the future) as business improves, bringing in greater income and reducing his debts.

In the meantime, the balance sheet gives Bill a tool to use when comparing the financial standing of his business this month against future months and years. It also keeps him current on what he owns, to whom he owes money, and his major sources of income.

The same procedure is used in developing a personal balance sheet, which possibly would be needed to establish credibility when applying for a loan. Assets would include furniture, automobiles, jewelry, a home, and other tangibles, while liabilities would consist of outstanding loans and other major debts.

Bank Statement Reconciliation

Another important step that Bill must handle monthly is reconciling his bank statement against his checkbook register. He simply marks off the checks in his register that have cleared per the bank statement, notes the deposits that have been credited, and deducts any service charges for the previous month from his balance.

Bill then adds up all the outstanding checks—those listed in his register that have not cleared by the closing date indicated on the bank statement—and *deducts* them from the balance indicated on his bank statement. He adds up any deposits that have not yet been credited to his account and then *adds* them to the balance, as follows.

Balance per bank statement	$7,953.44
Plus: Deposits not credited	+325.00
Minus: Outstanding checks	-115.90
New Balance	$8,162.54

The new balance figure should match that listed in his checkbook register and, in this case, it does. If, however, the statement and the register did not reconcile, Bill would have a customer representative at the bank review his statement and banking activity for the past month.

Notes

Key Points

Personal Thoughts

Additional Research

16

PRICING FOR PROFITS

One of the toughest problems facing small business owners is establishing prices that the market will bear and that will cover overhead and guarantee a profit.

Often new business owners give the business away to get sales, but this is not an advisable practice. Realistic pricing indicates your confidence in what you are selling, and if you value your service, so will the customer.

Today's consumer realizes that no one gets something worthwhile for nothing, so don't be afraid to establish prices that will work toward your profit goals.

Guidelines

Several factors must be taken into consideration when setting prices:

1. *The cost of goods sold.* In the case of a retail or wholesale operation, this is the amount originally paid for the goods. For a manufacturer, it is the cost of producing the goods.

2. *The nature of the product or service.* Uniqueness and demand come into play here. In the case of goods with a

stable level of demand, such as bread or auto repair, raising or lowering prices will have little effect. However, when demand is high for goods that are hard to get, the price can realistically be set anywhere the business owner wants. Such is often the case with restaurants featuring an exclusive or unusual menu.

3. *The competition.* It is important to recognize what your competition is charging, for often this will guide pricing within a certain region. However, if a competitor is charging what you feel is an unrealistic price—either more or less—for a product or service, you owe it to yourself to find out why. Then set your prices according to all of the factors outlined here. Even if your prices are higher than the competitor, consumers will pay the cost if you offer something special, such as a friendly atmosphere, convenient hours, follow-up service or maintenance, or some other benefit not provided by the competition.

4. *Your company policy.* This encompasses a number of things, including your location, your position in the marketplace, and additional services offered. It also takes into account your personal philosophy about business and your role in it.

5. *Market strategy.* Should you go for large volume at low prices or low volume at high prices? That is the bottom line in considering market strategy. As a small business owner, you will likely opt for low volume and higher prices, since the alternative involves having the resources, including labor, display room, distribution channels, etc., to move large volumes of product or perform major service tasks.

6. *Customers.* What will the market bear? In other words, what are your customers willing to pay for your products or services?

People expect prices that are fair; if you are planning to charge overinflated rates you had better be a topnotch salesperson or

have something so incredible and unusual to offer that the price won't matter.

Although there are differences between establishing prices for retail operations, wholesale products, manufacturing, and services, the basic formula for price setting is

Labor + Materials + Overhead + Profit Margin = Price

However, before setting prices on goods or services, it is extremely important to understand the concept of the break-even point. Many small business owners operate on an overall profit-loss basis without realizing the importance of cost accounting. Being aware of such factors as your break-even point, markup, and profit margin can tell you which areas of your business are profitable and which are causing a drain.

Understanding Break-even

The break-even point is the minimum amount you must charge in order to cover all expenses incurred for the production and promotion of your goods and/or services *without losing or making money.* In other words, any income that is above the break-even point is considered to be profit and anything below it is a loss.

To find your break-even point, you must first total all of your operating costs, including materials and labor, equipment lease or purchase payments, advertising, utilities, office supplies, and any incidentals such as gasoline, maintenance, and postage.

Generally, this is computed for a particular period of time, such as six months or a year. However, if your business is still in the early stages of operation, you can use the estimated figures on your projected expenses statement and guesstimate costs for materials and labor.

For example, the monthly expenses for your hypothetical cake-decorating business total $300.00. You want to know what the break-even point would be if you sold an average of 20 cakes per month. The calculation is as follows:

$$\frac{\$300.00 \ (expenses)}{20 \ cakes} = \$15.00$$

In order to break even, that is, to operate without losing money or realizing a profit, you must charge a minimum of $15.00 for each cake sold.

The same process can be used to analyze the break-even point on a weekly basis. First you determine your annual expenses by multiplying the $300.00 by 12 months, which would give you $3,600.00 per year.

The calculation to find the weekly break-even point is:

$$\frac{\$3,600.00 \ (expenses)}{52 \ weeks} = \$69.23$$

Therefore, you must earn $69.23 per week to operate the business without losing money and without realizing a profit.

Stay Informed

Knowing your break-even point is one of the greatest favors you can do for yourself as a business owner. It tells you how much you must charge for your products or services and is invaluable in setting prices to realize a profit.

Keep in mind, however, that the break-even point is a variable figure. Since it depends on production and overhead costs, plan to reevaluate periodically to make sure your prices reflect any changes.

Labor Costs

Labor costs, obviously, are the expenses incurred for the actual work done to manufacture or sell a product or to perform a service. Think of them as wages or salaries.

Small business owners often end up working for free because they fail to set a wage for themselves. Despite the fact that you will want to reinvest all of the income received back into the

business for a while, it is imperative that you establish a fixed salary amount for yourself when figuring operating expenses.

If you have set aside a survival fund for the first six months of operation, you may want to defer your salary until the business becomes solvent; however, you should still figure the amount into your expenses. Otherwise, you may find the prices you set are too low to justify making a profit from the onset.

It is much easier to set realistic prices from the beginning than it is to raise them later in an attempt to make up the difference. Remember, your time and skills are the cornerstone of your business, so think of paying yourself as you would any valuable employee.

Money is a sixth sense which makes it possible for us to enjoy the other five senses.

Richard Ney

17

INVENTORY AS INVESTMENT

Ask 100 small business owners what inventory means to them and more than 90 percent will tell you it's the merchandise they keep on hand to sell to their customers, or the materials and supplies stocked to produce goods or perform a service.

This is somewhat accurate, for inventory can and should be viewed as any supplies, raw materials, or finished goods used to generate a profit in your business. But it isn't the response that a savvy business owner would give.

Surprisingly, according to a recent study conducted by a leading consulting firm, less than 10 percent of a group of 500 entrepreneurs interviewed spoke of their inventory in terms of the *investment it represents;* an investment that can range from 15 to 25 percent of total operating capital.

It is because of this misunderstanding that many small business owners often fail to incorporate good inventory control practices into their regular management routine. Although they keep an eagle eye on every penny going through the books, they may totally overlook the cash tied up in their inventory.

Controlling Inventory

Inventory control can be a very simple, straightforward task if you implement a workable system from the beginning–preferably even *before* you start ordering and receiving goods. You will find that time really flies when you are self-employed, and it's very easy to postpone such tasks as inventory control until the inevitable day you find yourself facing this overwhelming job. Inventory control will give you valuable information about: (a) whether or not you are carrying too much or too little inventory based on, for example, items and prices preferred by your customers, or seasonal aspects, and (b) if you are realizing optimum economy determined by the costs of storage, taxes, handling, and the investment per unit.

The ideal situation is to maintain an inventory that is profitable because it turns over (comes in and goes out of the business) regularly, thereby lowering the cost of storing, displaying, and insuring it.

Although there are countless alumni of the school of hard knocks, there has not yet been a move to accredit that institution.

Sonya Rudikoff

There are several methods of inventory control that you can adopt, depending on your business. The main goal with each method, however, is to tell you how many items you have on hand and how many you need to meet your customer or production demands. It will also work toward lessening inventory shrinkage, which is generally the result of employee pilferage; customer theft; incorrect inventory storage; or sloppy record maintenance of items ordered, received, and used.

You can tell how many items you currently have by making an educated guess, which generally only works for businesses having a small, visible inventory that is relatively predictable. An example of the kind of business that could probably operate efficiently with this relaxed form of inventory control would be a

one- or two-person enterprise that monthly goes through a box of invoices and similar supplies available for a minimum amount at the discount office-supply store.

Other methods of inventory control are *the physical count,* which should be done at least once a year for tax purposes, or–the easiest and most efficient of them all–an *ongoing* record. Ideally, you should incorporate both systems by backing up periodic physical counts with a perpetual record.

To set up your perpetual system, simply create a file card or inventory sheet in a three-ring binder for each item in your inventory. Across the top of the card or sheet, list the following:

1. Item name and code number, if applicable

2. A description of the item

3. Where it is stored

4. The supplier's name, address, and phone number

5. Unit price (i.e., $12.95/dozen)

6. Your selling price if a retail item, or percentage of gross price of completed product, if used for manufacturing or service

7. The date you place an order

8. The number of items and the date they are received

Then, every time you sell or use an item, write it down and subtract it from the last balance. You should also indicate the reorder number, based on when and by how much you must replenish your stock.

The reorder number will be determined by such factors as the following:

1. The minimum cost per unit available from your supplier, including quantity discounts, preseason specials, and discounts for cash or quick payment

2. The delivery schedule–the delay between placing the order and receiving it

3. Economic and social trends that can affect the way an item is perceived by the public

For example, during a depressed or inflated economy, sales for leisure items typically drop. By keeping an eye on these factors, you can adjust your inventory needs accordingly and not get stuck with great quantities of items that you can't move.

After a while, you will be able to recognize at a glance which items are movers and which are simply taking up shelf space. When you reach this point, your ordering skills will become much more efficient and your investment in inventory will become a profitable proposition.

Notes

Key Points

Personal Thoughts

Additional Research

18

MAKING THE MOST OF YOUR TIME

A recent survey of small business owners indicated that one of the qualities they felt contributed the most to their success was organization. In conjunction with this is the fact that time management and basic organizational seminars continue to be the most popular offerings in adult education catalogs and business workshops around the country.

Time is money! It is vital to your success that you learn to manage your time and organize paperwork. This might sound rather simplistic, but you would be amazed at the number of small business owners who operate in a constant state of chaos.

Although we have seen a number of "A messy office is the sign of a creative mind" posters on entrepreneurs' office walls, it is a good bet that the holders of these signs can recount story after story of missing checks, lost orders, or misplaced files, which disrupted or halted the flow of business until they were located.

The survey respondents also stated that once they had learned to manage their time in both their personal and business lives and had set up guidelines for handling routine tasks, they felt more confident about accepting new challenges and making decisions.

The simple truth about getting organized is that it clears your mind for taking care of the nitty-gritty, profit-making aspects of

being in business—production and promotion. For example, just by setting aside a certain place in your work area to hold customer files and billing information, you have made one major step toward maximizing production. Knowing that all the supplies and materials needed to conduct your business are located in one place saves you both time and energy.

Making Time Work for You

Time management is the ability to take the hours we have available and use them to our advantage. Making lists of tasks to be done and giving them a priority rating is one of the best ways to avoid losing precious moments.

Keep a monthly calendar handy to help you keep track of major commitments, important dates, and appointments. Try to avoid using it for notations of daily work in progress, carryover tasks, or other things that are best suited for inclusion on your daily and weekly lists. There are several other ideas you can easily incorporate into your working lifestyle that will maximize your productivity.

Work Smart

Handle the jobs you find most difficult or cumbersome during peak performance time. If you are a morning person and find that making telephone calls to potential customers is one of your least favorite tasks, make those calls first thing in the morning when you are feeling fresh and energetic. Then organize the rest of the day's tasks accordingly.

Set Realistic Daily Goals for Yourself

Just because you are the key employee, don't try to do everything at once. Learn just how much work you can accept and expect to accomplish in a given period of time and allow yourself to turn down work if it seems like it will be too much for you to handle.

Positive Reinforcement

When you work alone, as many small business owners do when getting their businesses off the ground, there generally aren't many people around to support or praise your work...and everyone needs strokes! Remember that a customer's praises are proof that you are doing a good job.

Reward Yourself

Sometimes it is easy to forget that you are important to the business—you *are* the business. So treat yourself to a special dinner now and then or plan an evening where you go out to a movie or do something else that has absolutely nothing to do with business. Remind yourself that this is your reward for accomplishing certain goals for your business. It will help to keep your spirits high.

Don't Procrastinate

Don't put off doing tasks that must be done. If you constantly let some tasks slide because you don't enjoy doing them or they are boring and time-consuming, you will soon find yourself back-logged and unable to catch up. The effects of procrastination may not be obvious until you are faced with a deadline and, at that point, you will realize that you are working at less than maximum efficiency using the wrong supplies, feeling tense, and being hassled by minor problems that could have been avoided. Even when business is slow and it seems that there could be little harm done by taking a day off to go to the beach, be sure to complete all your required tasks before closing up shop.

Limit Personal Phone Calls

Ask friends and relatives not to call during established business hours. These friendly calls not only eat into productive time, they tie up the line when an important client may be trying to get in touch with you. The same holds true with visitors. If you are self-employed, friends and family often feel that you are not really "working" and that they can stop by anytime to chat. Explain that you will be happy to visit with them at some other time and be sure to tell them why so there aren't any ill feelings.

Obviously, there will be times when unavoidable situations arise, such as an emergency or an unexpected problem. Take these into consideration by estimating how long a project will take and then adding a bit of extra time to give yourself some leeway.

Delegate

If you find that you absolutely cannot handle a certain aspect of the business, such as your own bookkeeping, for example, don't labor over the task—you will end up wasting a great deal of time and could make some serious mistakes. Admit to yourself that the task is just not your strong point and make arrangements to have someone else do it.

Learn to Say "No"

One of the hardest things for most people to do is to say "no." Even when we realize that helping a friend out on a special project will cost valuable time, we often agree to do it because we hate to say no. What we do is justify our acceptance by assuring ourselves that saying yes will put us in the position of meeting a lot of potential customers. The reality is that using that time to make phone calls or a sales call for your own business will probably result in a paying customer, not just a potential contact.

Minimize Business Meetings

Before setting up a formal meeting, which can be very time consuming, see if you can take care of the matter by phone or through the mail. If a meeting can't be avoided, make sure you specify a time limit to encourage people to get down to business. Another time-saving device for meetings is to work up an agenda that outlines exactly what has to be discussed to avoid idle chit-chat and unnecessary diversions.

Plan Your Time

When you have to run errands, plan them for a sensible time, such as in the morning when traffic is light. Plan to do as many things as possible in one trip, outlining the stops you must make so they follow a sequential order.

Notes

Key Points

Personal Thoughts

Additional Research

19

GETTING DOWN TO BUSINESS

To check out your clients thoroughly, you should make up a form for them to fill out, which should include banking information. When an order comes in, immediately make up a work order. Contracts facilitate cash-flow management. The majority of a firm's clients are on contract. And, of course, getting and keeping contracts demands top service and consistency. Good bookkeeping skills come in handy as business increases!

The next step is to bill the client for services performed by your temps. Most agencies attach a copy of the temps' signed time sheets to the invoice. The temps must be regularly supplied with time sheets.

The time sheets basically bear the name of the client company and the temp's name and social security number. The temp worker's hours on the job are recorded, and the time sheet is signed by both the temp and his or her immediate supervisor on the job.

Although you have many services and responsibilities required of you, there are certain things you must require in return. While you do your best to service the customer, you should uphold certain standards. You must make it part of your normal course of business to ask the customer for bank references. And, if you find from your employee that a client has misrepresented a job, don't

hesitate to discuss it with the client, but never in an accusing tone, of course.

Keeping a File

Another part of the day-to-day operation of an agency involves good record keeping. Keep a file on each temp, including the temp's tests, scores, application, a photocopy of the social security card and driver's license, and comments from the person who interviewed the temp.

In addition, a record of each job the temp has been sent out on and his or her performance in that job should be maintained. Also make it part of your routine to keep track of client records. Work-order copies should be kept and, of course, all bookkeeping should be in order.

It is not enough to have great qualities, we should also have management of them.

La Rochefoucauld

Starting Small Is Fine

Many of the big names in temporary help services started out quite small, some with just two or three people in a tiny office. Many of the women we spoke to got started in the temp help industry as a side business and now are realizing profits of between $75,000 and $300,000 per year.

One agency that specializes in domestic temps is quite successful handling a large volume of business with the efforts of just two people—the owner and one employee. However, it is advisable to hire more people when the business warrants it.

The Holloways did this. They now have four employees who help with the interviewing, telephone answering, and paperwork. Cindy Holloway sees this as the only way to build the agency and grow.

"The profit you can make from an agency depends in part on the amount of people you have hired to interview and so forth,"

she explained. "The best people to hire are those with marketing and sales skills and who are money motivated."

Many of the employees of temporary help agencies are given a base salary and a commission on any new business they draw in. Besides sales and interviewing personnel, you will also want to hire a receptionist.

Managing the Business

Offering your clients top service involves finding out their needs and meeting those needs appropriately. For example, if a company calls you for a temp with executive secretarial skills, you will need to send them someone with shorthand, good typing, and spelling skills. It pays to find out exactly what skills will be needed for each position.

It is very important that the person you send out who you say has these skills really does have them! This is where good and thorough testing shows. Never determine that an applicant has a certain skill just because they say so. It is up to you to send your clients temps who have proven their skills by adequate testing.

Matching the Temp to the Job

On the other hand, no client appreciates being sent—and billed for—an overqualified temp. It could make a businessperson most unhappy to pay $10 per hour for an executive secretary when a $6 per hour receptionist was all that was needed.

The temporary help business is a service business, and it is your responsibility to see that your temps meet the client's expectations. Many agencies guarantee that the temp will be satisfactory or they will replace the temp free of charge.

Most agency owners call the client to see if the temp has arrived on time and is performing satisfactorily. This is a good public relations touch and also can help spot problems right away.

Going the Extra Mile

Companies will keep returning to the agency that gives them good service, which includes the ability and willingness to go that extra

mile. For example, when a business becomes short handed because of an employee's illness, you may be asked to get them a temp within minutes. A cheerful attitude and some "stick-to-it-iveness" on the telephone are invaluable in such cases.

Your reputation is all important in the temp service business. Much of your business may come by word-of-mouth. So good service not only helps you keep your clients, it will also ensure new business.

20

HIRING EMPLOYEES

Good temps are the heart of your business. Without them you will never keep your clients happy. So it makes good sense to offer your temps good service as well as your clients. You should tell your temps to let you know what they think of the job you have assigned them to. Most agencies want to know if the temp is unhappy; perhaps the temp can be reassigned. This way, the temp will not get discouraged and go to another agency, which is something you want to avoid if the temp is a good one. Also, unhappy temps may not do the best job for your client. In addition, you should tell your temps to let you know if the job is not what they expected it to be.

Knowledge is of two kinds. We know a subject ourselves or we know where we can find information on it.

Samuel Johnson

For instance, if the company asks for a receptionist, and you are paying the temp a receptionist's wages, but the temp is asked to do a lot of statistical typing, you need to make amends. Either you

could bill the company the higher statistical typing rate and pay the temp more, or if the temp really cannot or does not want to do the typing, you should send someone else.

In addition, it pays to give feedback. Most people thrive on praise, and temps are no different. If the company says the temp did a good job, tell the temp so.

You must also be responsible for paying temps in a timely fashion, to keep them happy with your service. Usually temps are paid weekly.

Handling Complaints

Your temps are expected to do a good job for the client. If you receive more than one complaint about a temp it may be time to do something about it. Of course, you will need to take into consideration any mitigating factors. Was it really the temp's fault?

Maybe that particular customer was impossible to please. But you cannot afford to risk your good name in this business. One agency owner advises, when choosing temps, "Be cautious, and take nothing on face value. Be a real skeptic. You need a good sense of people to succeed in this business. The only thing you have going for you is your reputation. If you don't have the right people to fill jobs, don't send them! Just bringing in business is not enough. You have to consider what will profit the company in the end."

This agency owner says that when she bought her business, she was paying for the lists of good clients and temps. But most important to her were the lists of "bad" clients and temps!

Many agencies have a special "inactive" file for temps who have had too many complaints. Because of possible lawsuits or unpleasantness, agencies don't tell a temp they are being "blacklisted." Instead a counselor or agency owner will just tell the temp, "Sorry, we just don't have anything."

Inactive Files

There is also another kind of inactive file agencies keep, one that is really "inactive." The temps in this file are satisfactory workers

who have moved on to permanent jobs or moved out of the area, or are unavailable for placement for some other reason. But smart agencies know that the work force is ever changeable. Perhaps these people will move back to town or want to work temporary again. Storing their files could save a lot of time and money in retesting and interviewing.

The Day-to-Day Routine

Once you have your office set up with the bare essentials, including typewriters and phones, the day-to-day work at a temp agency is pretty straightforward. You and your employees will spend a lot of time on the phone, calling clients and calling temps to fill jobs. You also will spend a lot of time setting appointments for prospective temps to come in and be tested.

Working With the Temps

You or your interviewers will spend a great deal of time interviewing and testing temps. The types of tests you give will depend a great deal on the type of placement your agency specializes in. Some general tests for clerical workers include spelling, math, typing, and word processing.

References should definitely be checked. You are also required by law to have proof of citizenship or right to work in the country. Most agencies photocopy the applicant's driver's license and social security card.

Interviewlng the temp is an important job in determining what types of companies and types of jobs the temp likes and/or is suited for. For instance, if a temp says he or she does not own a suit, you will need to place that person in companies with a casual dress code.

Aftcr a temp checks out, and is ready to be sent out on jobs, you will need to give him or her a couple of time sheets to take on jobs. The sheets are to be signed by the client and returned to you. You should have time sheets with three copies: one for you, one for the client to keep, and one for the temp to keep. Many agencies send a new time sheet to the temp in each pay envelope.

Tips on Hiring Employees

♦ ***Recruit on a consistent basis.*** Even if you are fully staffed, interview potential employees regularly so you have names to draw on in the event that someone quits suddenly or is unable to show up for any reason. Men and women are equally suited for employment in your business.

♦ ***Create a sense of team spirit.*** Let your employees know they are vital to the success of the business. Although you can't afford to be friends with everyone, do let them know you are available for moral support and compassionate about their feelings. Some owners hold monthly meetings so that employees can share their experiences on the job and talk about more effective ways to handle clients or problems they encounter on the road. Communication is a necessary factor in successful employee relations because the business is so personal.

♦ ***Be flexible.*** The majority of your workers will probably have family responsibilities. If you are willing to arrange work schedules around individual needs, your employees will be appreciative and more likely to make an effort to please you and the clients.

As soon as you feel you are ready, place an ad in the classified ads of the local newspaper to recruit potential workers. Also register with your local state unemployment office. Students, who will only be available on a seasonal basis, can be found by contacting the placement offices of major colleges and universities. In addition, you can often find excellent candidates in friends or family of current employees.

The Benefits of Happy Employees

Personnel management is a time-consuming job for the business owner. However, paying attention to the needs of your employees and working to gain their trust and maintain their loyalty can do nothing but benefit your business.

The attitude of your employees about your management techniques plays an important part in building and maintaining your reputation in the business world. If employees are treated fairly and with respect, their job satisfaction will be reflected in the way they do their jobs.

This is something that can truly keep you ahead of the competition; a loyal, efficient, and enthusiastic group of workers is one of your most effective forms of public relations, so never scrimp when it comes to keeping your employees happy. A few important rules of thumb in dealing with employees include the following:

- ◆ *Never expect an employee to do something you wouldn't do.* This is why training new recruits yourself is such a good idea; it shows them that you are willing and able to step in and do anything that needs to be done.

- ◆ *Listen to your employees.* Talk to your staff regularly and incorporate any ideas they have whenever feasible. Remember that they have firsthand knowledge about how certain aspects of the job are done and might know if they can be done more efficiently. Suggestions that work for the good of the company should be rewarded with a bonus.

- ◆ *Take the time to talk about business standards and practices.* Make sure everyone knows exactly what is expected of them. Outline duties and responsibilities on the job and schedule regular reviews to ensure that they are constantly met. If you find it necessary to talk to an employee about work habits, do it in private. And do not criticize; offer constructive ways that performance can be improved.

- ◆ *Treat each employee as an individual.* When someone seems to be having personal problems that are interfering with his or her work, be willing to allow him or her time off without penalty to take care of the situation. An employee plagued with problems may carry them to work, and this could have a negative effect on productivity. It is much better to get someone to fill in until the regular employee is operating at full efficiency again.

Notes

Organizational Ideas

Personnel Requirements

Recruiting Techniques

21

ADVERTISING YOUR BUSINESS

More than 150 years ago, Thomas Macaulay, a British historian and statesman, said, "Advertising is to business what steam is to industry. [They provide] the same propelling power."

Few in business would argue with Macaulay's observation—it is as true today as it was when steam was the driving force behind industry. But the question remains, "How do you get the most out of your advertising dollar?" The answer is to

1. Know your customer
2. Target your market
3. Understand the basics of advertising

This chapter provides an overview of various aspects of advertising, including how to use circulation figures to figure your cost per thousand (CPM) and how to create ads that will bring results.

What Is Advertising?

Advertising informs the public about

♦ Who you are
♦ What kind of business you operate

♦ How they can buy your products or services

♦ Why they should come to you

Before you even open the doors of your business, you should start thinking about your advertising program—how much money you can afford to spend, where your dollars will be best spent, and how to structure your campaign.

Decide what kind of results you want. Are you looking for immediate sales or ongoing recognition? What kind of customers are you hoping to attract? Are you emphasizing price, service, workmanship, or something unique? Once you have answered these questions, your decision as to the best type of advertising for the allotted dollars will be easier to make.

There are three basic types of advertising that you will be most interested in during the first few years of your business.

Start-up Advertising

This includes your business cards and stationery, announcement flyers and brochures, and your initial ads in newspapers or other publications. At this point, your main focus will be on telling people where you are located and what you can offer them.

Ongoing Advertising

Once the business is up and running, it will be vital to your success to institute a regular advertising campaign that is well thought out and—this is the key—consistent. Your goal at this point is to attract new clients, obtain repeat business from existing customers, and enhance your reputation.

Appearance Advertising

After you have reached the point where your business is on steady ground and you're showing increased profits every year, you can afford to dabble in "institutional advertising," as it is called in the trade. This is where you pick up the tab to send a dozen kids to the rodeo when it comes to town, or you sponsor a float in the local parade and, in return, get your name listed on the program or on a banner in the parade. This is primarily name recognition only

and, while every little bit is helpful, by the time you can afford it, you probably will be in pretty good shape anyway.

Yellow Pages

Check with the phone company and find out when the next directory is coming out and what the deadline is for a Yellow Pages ad. Buy the biggest ad you think you can afford. You will be billed monthly by the phone company as part of your regular bill. The cost can be up to several hundred dollars per month, so buy your space carefully. Have the ad designed by a professional graphic artist to ensure that it stands apart from the rest.

The size and appearance of your ad make a very big difference in the number of calls you can expect and the type of customers who call. Don't advertise that you're the cheapest in town—remember that your best customers are looking for quality employees not bargains.

Plan ahead at least well enough to know what your business phone number will be, and try to open at about the same time that the new directory comes out.

"Timing the start-up of your business with the publication of the Yellow Pages is vital to your business," reveals Cindy Holloway. "When Larry and I first started we had just missed publication! It might have almost been advisable to wait and start the business with the new Yellow Pages! But we didn't. To compensate, I just had to send out massive mailing–thousands of letters to clients, telling about us and what we had to offer."

Cindy advises a reasonably sized ad as being most effective. She says the psychology of overdoing it can be negative. "It's just psychology," she explains. "Companies are interested in agencies that are solvent and well established. They may not look at the display ad which is screaming out for business."

Referrals and Repeat Business

You will know which clients are happy with your service. First, they will tell you what a great temp you've assigned to them and will call you when they need another and, second, they may say

something to the effect, "I'm going to pass the word along about you and your service."

However, if they don't offer to pass your name along, it is perfectly legitimate to give them a slight push in that direction. An informal note, sent out within a day or two of their using the service, does the job nicely.

Sample Follow-Up Mailer

We Enjoyed Serving You!

Thank you for using Quality Temps. We hope your experience with us was as pleasant as expected. Please remember us the next time you need a professionally trained, qualified employee, and the best service available in the temporary help business. If you or any of your coworkers have overload work or a permanent employee who is on sick leave or vacation, please call us first. We look forward to serving you again.

Call 555-1212 for Top Rated Temps!

Reaching a Specialized Market

Speciality advertising works extremely well in this business. Specialty advertising refers to the matches, pens, desk calendars, and similar items that have a company's name printed on them. Every time you use the item, you think about the firm, even if it is subconscious.

Investigate the kind of items you can have printed by visiting a specialty advertising representative (listed in the phone book under "Advertising-Specialties"). Pens, oversized plastic paper clips, and desk notepads are appropriate for a temporary help service to use as handouts.

Classified Advertising

Classified ads can be crucial to business revenue—an inexpensive way to sell your service and hire employees. Don't underestimate the power of classified ads. Many major corporations use classified ads even though they have sizable budgets available for display advertising. There are several reasons for this.

1. Classified ads are an extremely reliable testing ground for new products, services, and ideas. Although it is true that people who typically read the classified section are a different group from those who scan display ads, they are considered to be responsive and, therefore, can give you a very good idea of whether or not you have placed your ad in the appropriate publication.

2. A short, well-written classified ad placed in the right publication and under the proper category can be a low-cost method of advertising that guarantees solid returns.

3. If a company is trying to establish a mailing list, a classified ad that features an "Inquiry" statement, such as "Send name and address for free details (or a brochure)," is a good way to build up a file of qualified buyers' names. And they can be considered qualified buyers because it takes time, energy, and the cost of a postage stamp for them to get your free information. By writing to you they have stated their interest.

4. Classified ads are inexpensive. With careful planning, you should be able to get broad-based coverage without putting a dent in your operating capital.

Here's an example:

Sample Classified Advertisement

Need Office Help? Think Quality Temps for your overload and emergency fill-in. You deserve the very best! Call 555-1212 for a quote and free booklet on hiring.

Use classified ads to attract qualified temporary workers as well. You should run this ad on a continual basis in every possible local publication to breed familiarity among potential temps. Although they may not respond the first, the fifth, or even the tenth time they see the ad, chances are good that they will remember your name when they're ready to register with a temporary help agency.

Sample Classified Ad for Temps

We've got a job for you! Quality Temps guarantees high-paying assignments tailored to your skills. Legal, medical, technical, secretarial, accounting. Call Mary at 555-1212 for an appointment.

Direct Mail

Keep in mind that you promote your business through publicity, advertising, direct mail, or personal contact. Direct mail is often the best, because a prospective client can read your "approach" letter at his or her convenience. This letter should include the following:

1. The reason you are writing
2. Your experience
3. Your facilities
4. Special features
5. Financial advantages of using your service

Display Advertising

Don't dismiss the possibility of running small display ads on a seasonal basis, even though they are more expensive than classified advertising. Focus on promoting through display advertising during specific times of the year when you know that certain markets will need them.

Choose your publications wisely, concentrating on related trade publications. Consider offering an incentive, such as a 10

percent discount if customers bring in the ad. This will help you track responses and plan future display ad campaigns.

As with all types of advertising, it is important to define your market when getting ready to place a display ad. Your main goal is to select a publication that will reach the audience you want, then create a specific, attention-getting ad that appeals to that target group.

To Write or Not to Write

Writing display ad copy is not for the inexperienced. Although it is possible to learn how to put ideas and words together that will pull the results you desire, it is recommended that you hire a copywriter if you have any qualms about producing an ad.

However, if you are confident that you can develop your own ad, remember that it must build identity through the use of carefully planned words and design. Glance through newspapers and magazines to find ads that catch your eye. Most likely, the ones that stand out have a memorable logo, effective use of space, or an unusual headline that leads you into the body of the ad.

These are ads you should refer to as samples when designing your own.

When planning your ad, keep the following elements in mind:

1. **Visibility.** Your ad may be surrounded by many others, so design it so that it will immediately attract the reader's attention.

2. **Boldness.** Use large art and/or a bold headline as a focal point.

3. **Simplicity.** Don't overwhelm the reader with too many fine details. The ad's main point is lost and so is the reader's attention. This is particularly true in a small ad.

4. **White space.** Just because you have, say, a four-by-six-inch space to work with, it isn't necessary to fill it up. In fact, white space is a necessary component in assuring your ad will be read.

5. **Use simple-to-read typefaces.** Two that are popular are Times Roman and Bookman, which are known as serif

typefaces because of the tiny strokes at the tops and bottoms of the letters.

Sans-serif (without strokes) typefaces, such as Helvetica, are fine for ads containing only a few words, but are difficult for the eye to follow when there is a lot of text.

Also, be sure that the type is large enough; generally nothing smaller than 10-point type should be used. If type is too small to read, it will simply be ignored.

Design and Typesetting

It isn't necessary to be a great artist to create an ad, especially these days with the availability of a variety of impressive graphic software programs. In addition, you can buy cut-out-and-transfer (press-on) letters in different typefaces, symbols, borders, and designs through graphic-art-supply companies. Most word processing programs also contain computer graphics that can dress up your ad at a low cost.

If you feel uncomfortable about laying out your ad so it has eye appeal, consider hiring an art student to handle the job for a prearranged fee or as a school assignment. (Talk with the head of the art department to see if there is a work/study for credit program.) Just be sure to review the student's work prior to making a commitment.

Also, check with the advertising department of the newspaper or magazine you are planning to advertise in. There may be graphic artists or designers on staff who will work on the layout for you. In fact, there are still newspapers in the country that offer full service, from ad concept to design work, at a minimal charge to their advertising clients.

Advertising is the greatest art form
of the twentieth century.

Marshall McLuhan

Publications work on tight deadlines, so be sure you start the process early enough to get a proof copy of your ad back in time to make any corrections. You can imagine the anguish in seeing your ad appear with the wrong address. Although the publication would probably do a "make-good" for you and run a corrected ad at no charge, the damage has already been done. The final responsibility for the ad rests with you, so, as with any other aspect of your business, plan ahead.

Tracking Ad Response

Some customers will tell you that they saw your ad and might even let you know what they liked or disliked about it if you ask them. Even so, you should develop other methods for determining if your advertising is working.

One very simple way is to include a coupon for something in the ad and then count the number of coupons you get within a certain test period after the ad runs. There is one major problem with this, however. Even the most well-intentioned people often cut coupons, file them away in a "safe" place, and totally forget about them.

So, although you will be able to gauge response to some degree, be aware that many of the people who come into or call your business have probably seen the coupon but simply mislaid it or are not the kind of folks who use them.

Predicting Ad Response

There is a standardized formula in advertising that provides a barometer for predicting how much response can be expected from either a display ad or a classified ad. The formula states that you will see one-half of the total responses from an ad within a certain period of time after receiving your first inquiry or order.

For an ad run in a daily newspaper, the period of time is three days; for a weekly newspaper or magazine, it is six days; within fifteen days for a monthly publication, and within twenty-five days when running in a bimonthly. Although there will be exceptions to this rule, it does give you a base from which to track response.

Determining Your Cost Per Thousand

The cost per thousand (CPM) equation helps you develop a cost-effective campaign. Basically, it tells you what your ad cost per thousand readers will be. Most publications will provide a CPM comparison upon request (some include it in their Media Kits), but you can figure it out for yourself with just a few facts from publications that you are exploring as advertising vehicles.

For convenience sake, CPM equations are typically based on the rate of a full-page, black-and-white ad. You simply divide the full-page rate by the thousands of circulation. It is important that you get the circulation, *not* the readership, because magazines and newspapers typically claim that their readership is 2 to 50 percent higher because of "pass-along" of the publication to friends or relatives.

For example, if a certain newspaper is charging $2,000 for a full-page ad, and it claims the true circulation is 200,000, you will be paying $10 per 1,000 readers for your ad space. Another specialized publication's full-page rate may be $1,000 with a circulation of 50,000. The cost per 1,000 readers will be much higher—$20 per 1,000, but it might be worth it if, for example, you have a unique product or service that is geared to an exclusive market.

Benefits of Paid Circulation

It is also important to know that publications with a paid circulation generally have a readership that is more inclined to respond to advertising. This is because of the simple fact that they are a captive audience who have taken the time to *order* the publication. This is especially valuable if you have a product or service that you're planning to market through mail-order channels.

You can find circulation, readership demographics, advertising rates, and other important information about a number of publications (especially those with national distribution) through *Standard Rate and Data Service (SRDS),* available through the research desk of your local library.

The Advertising Research Foundation and the Association of Business Publishers conducted a study to determine the impact of

advertising on the sale of products. Several different products were used for the study, and each was advertised for a twelve-month period in an appropriate publication. The results were interesting, but not surprising to anyone who has ever utilized a solid advertising campaign in promoting a business.

- More advertising meant more sales.

- Determining results from an ad campaign generally took four to six months. One or two insertions do not indicate viable results.

- Color in advertisements dramatically increased response and sales.

- A well-developed ad campaign keeps on working for a year and sometimes even longer in publications with high "keep" appeal.

Knowledge and belief in your product, faith in yourself, and respect for your customers are the keys to successfully building your future. As you go about starting and establishing your business, remember the word "profit." This alone should give you the necessary motivation to get out there and confidently tell the world what you have to offer.

Sample Display Ad for Clients

QUALITY TEMPS
PERSONNEL SERVICE

*We place temps for a day,
a week, a month, or longer.
All applicants carefully screened
and tested for your convenience.*

555-1212

Office Staffing
- Reception
- Secretarial
- Word Processing
- Bookkeeping

Professional
- Legal
- Accounting
- Architecture
- Medical

Sample Recruiting Ad

QUALITY TEMPS
PERSONNEL SERVICE

Become a Career Temp and Enjoy

- Fabulous Benefits
- Flexible Work Schedule
- Excellent Pay and Bonuses

- Top-Ranked Employers
- Free Specialized Training
- Permanent Placement

Call today for an appointment.

555-1212

Notes

Key Points

Personal Thoughts

Additional Research

22

PROMOTION AND PUBLIC RELATIONS

Informing the public about your business through the use of business cards, brochures, mailing pieces, catalogs, and specialty items (calendars, pens, and T-shirts imprinted with your company name) is a form of advertising that is known as promotion; what you do over and above your paid advertising and promotion that help build your image and keep your business in the public consciousness are referred to as public relations. There is a fine line between the two, and they can make or break your business if not addressed.

There are many clever ways to extend the effectiveness of your advertising and promotional dollars, as illustrated in the following examples.

A Little Creativity Goes a Long Way

The owner of a pet grooming business leaves a business card and a brochure featuring a 20 percent discount coupon everywhere he goes. When he is running errands, he always takes a handful of brochures with him to hand to store clerks, gas station attendants, and even food servers he runs into during the day.

If he sees a car with a dog in it, or one with a bumper sticker announcing the owner's affection for a pet, he slips a brochure

under the windshield wiper. Does it work? Absolutely. He claims that 45 percent of his new business comes from the recipients of his handouts, and the majority of them become regular customers.

Another business owner who operates a small walking tour service in her beachside town sends out a one-page quarterly newsletter featuring historical and other facts about the area to everyone who has ever taken the tour. She includes a $10 coupon that can be redeemed by former clients or their guests.

She states that many of her clients are local residents who send their out-of-town visitors on her walking tour, simply because she makes sure they are aware that she is still in business and generates enthusiasm through the newsletter.

Advertisements contain the only truths to be relied on in a newspaper.

Thomas Jefferson

Charity Tie-ins

Other ideas you might consider include promoting humanitarian outreach. For example, for every ten products a customer buys or every tenth time a customer uses your service, you donate a predetermined amount of money to a local charity. You can easily keep track of customers' purchases by punching a hole at the edge of a card designed by you or your printer strictly for that purpose.

When you are ready to present the check to the particular charity, make sure the chairperson of the organization is there to accept it and be sure to contact the local press and invite them to the "event." In most cases, you'll receive free coverage.

According to successful entrepreneurs, free giveaways are the most successful promotions. You can order items such as pens, pencils, notepads, and calendars, just to name a few, with your name and phone number printed on them to give to people. Every time recipients use the item, they will automatically think of you! Another idea is to offer one day's free temporary help service as a

prize in a community raffle. Check under "Advertising Specialties" in the Yellow Pages for prices and more ideas.

Networking

Check out local business-owner groups and the chamber of commerce in your area. Pay your membership dues and join as many groups as possible. Membership in these organizations offers you the opportunity to meet people who might use your service and will, at bare minimum, tell others about you once they know you, feel comfortable with you, and understand what you are offering. You will also be given a listing in the group's directory, generally under your specific category.

And, as is so often the case, members are prone to supporting others involved with their group. It is quite possible that members with compatible businesses will put a stack of your cards or brochures on their counter or in their referral file. In return, you may be able to promote their businesses to your customers. This is the true meaning of networking.

The directory also gives you bona-fide access to an instant mailing list, which you can use to send out promotional flyers or brochures. Participating in the organization's events and the willingness, for example, to speak at functions about your area of specialization will let people know that you are community-minded. This involvement will work to project a positive image for you and your business.

Customer Service

One of the most overlooked areas in promoting business is the way we create an impression when dealing with the public on a one-to-one basis. The ageless philosophy that the customer is always right and comes first has, it seems, gotten lost in the shuffle in these days of fast-paced transactions.

As a small business owner, you can be sure that customers will flock to you if you make them feel important. It is as easy as greeting them warmly (instruct your employees, if you have them, to do the same), maintaining a courteous attitude, and inviting them to come back soon—even if they have not spent any money.

Remember that word travels fast, and if you create an atmosphere that makes all your customers feel special, you can be sure they will tell their friends and neighbors.

Reminder Cards

Sending regular "thinking-of-you" cards to your past and present clientele is especially effective with service businesses. Again, it assures the customer that you are friendly, reliable, and conscientious—real pluses for your credibility.

Free Publicity

Free publicity also comes under the category of public relations. This includes newspaper, magazine, radio, and television interviews that feature interesting or unusual facts about you and your business.

As any newspaper reporter or talk-show host will tell you, everybody has a story to tell. The key is to get the media to zero in on yours and make it available to the public. If you have trouble deciding on a unique angle for your story, invite several friends over for a brainstorming session to create a newsworthy item.

Use your imagination to explore the creative possibilities of your business venture. And then look at your personal story. Perhaps you have completely switched fields with your new business: There's a story with a strong slant toward risk-taking. Maybe you have successfully turned a hobby into a business venture, created a unique product, or developed a new twist on an old theme. These all qualify as human-interest stories. Newspaper and magazine editors like them almost as much as their readers enjoy them.

Once you have your story angle, call the managing editor or the feature editor of your local newspaper. Give him or her a brief description of who you are and what business you are in. Say that you will be sending out a press release (see sample) and would be happy to arrange an interview at a convenient time.

Sample Press Release

FOR IMMEDIATE RELEASE CALL 555-1212 FOR DETAILS

Quality Temps Open for Business

Mary Smith announces the grand opening of Quality Temps in Anytown Mall. She and her staff guarantee top-quality employees to fill in for vacationing or ill personnel or to handle overload work in the following areas: legal, medical, and secretarial services including word processing and bookkeeping; and marketing, retail, and technical services.

"I worked as a career temp for three years after moving to Anytown," says Smith. "It was such an exciting opportunity—learning about different businesses, meeting hundreds of wonderful people, and being able to tailor my work schedule around the needs of my young family—that I decided to get into the placement end of the business."

Smith claims that local businesses are using temporary employees with greater regularity these days as a way to beat inflation and reduce the effects of burnout. On the other hand, it has become the choice of many secretaries, bookkeepers, and professionals who prefer not to be tied down and enjoy the challenge of new business opportunities. A number of temps, she continued, go on to become permanent employees when they find a match of salary and job responsibility.

For further information on hiring temps or becoming a Quality Temp, call 555-1212 for a free copy of Smith's booklet, "The Temp Revolution."

Invite journalists to visit your place of business to get a firsthand look at what you are doing and how you do it. Do the same with program directors or talk-show hosts at local and regional television and radio stations.

If, on the first attempt, your presentation fails to result in an article, follow up in three to six months, possibly with a new story angle. In the meantime, however, send out regular press releases

announcing new developments with your business—the grand opening, special events, details on your business philosophy, extra services, and features.

Even if they don't run a full story on you, there is a good possibility you could be included in a feature story about local entrepreneurs or people in related businesses.

An Effective Ad Campaign

All of the methods outlined earlier, along with any others you may develop, will keep your name in the consumer's mind. The effectiveness of an advertising and/or publicity campaign can be measured by conducting a simple marketing survey with new customers. Simply make it standard practice to ask each customer where he or she heard about you and your business.

Keep a tally of the responses in a notebook. A periodic review will give you hints of where to allocate future advertising funds. If, for example, the majority of your customers are being drawn from your display ad in the local newspaper, keep it going on a steady basis. The same principle applies to classified, direct-mail, or word-of-mouth advertising.

The justification for investing in advertising and promotion is time. If you attempted to contact all of the people who read ads and press-release material in newspapers, or those who listen to talk shows, you would never have time to conduct your business.

The advertisement is one of the most interesting and difficult of modern literary forms.

Aldous Huxley

Time is money! As a small business owner, you will want to devote as much attention as possible to the production end of your venture and let your advertising and promotion bring in the customers.

Notes

Key Points

Personal Thoughts

Additional Research

Appendix: Resources

Associations and Agencies

Small Business Associations & Government Agencies

American Marketing Association
250 South Wacker Drive, Suite 200
Chicago, IL 60606-5819

Marketing publications available to nonmembers.

Bureau of the Census
Washington, DC 20233

Statistical data.

Chambers of Commerce
Consult Yellow Pages. Services vary among chambers but may include advice, support, workshops or seminars, local business news, and other services for small businesses.

Council of Better Business Bureaus
4200 Wilson Boulevard, Suite 800
Arlington, VA 22203

Ask for a listing of their "Booklets on Wise Buying."

Dun & Bradstreet
299 Park Avenue
New York, NY 10171

Send for the booklet "This is Dun & Bradstreet," an overview of publications and services.

Internal Revenue Service (IRS)
1-800-829-1040 General tax assistance
1-800-829-3676 Forms and publications

See the government section of your phone book for address and phone of the local office. The IRS publishes a variety of books and brochures that are useful to owners of small businesses. Each year the IRS publishes *Tax Guide for Small Business*.

International Franchise Association
1350 New York Avenue NW
Washington, DC 20005

Regulation and information on franchises.

Local Planning Agencies
See the government section of your phone book for address and phone of the local office. Source of information on zoning and future development locations.

Minority Business Development Agency
Office of Public Affairs
Department of Commerce
Washington, DC 20230

National Association for the Self-Employed
PO Box 612067
DFW Airport, TX 75261-2067

National Association of Women Business Owners
600 South Federal Street
Chicago, IL 60605

National Minority Business Council

235 East 42nd Street
New York, NY 10017

Bimonthly newsletter for small and minority businesses.

National Small Business United

1155 15th Street NW, Suite 710
Washington, DC 20005

Send for information on federal legislation.

Occupational Safety & Health Administration (OSHA)

Department of Labor
200 Constitution Avenue NW
Washington, DC 20210

Employment regulations.

Office of Information and Public Affairs

U.S. Department of Labor
200 Constitution Avenue NW
Washington, DC 20210

Request publications list regarding employment.

Service Corps of Retired Executives (SCORE)

See Small Business Administration.

Small Business Administration

1441 L Street NW
Washington, DC 20416

The SBA is the primary source of federal governmental assistance for small businesses. In addition to providing financing for many small businesses, it provides a number of services for free or at a small cost. SBA regional offices routinely conduct free or low-cost small business workshops. The SBA also offers many helpful publications as well as the following hotlines:

SBA Answer Desk

Recorded information on a variety of topics

1-800-827-5722

SBA Online

A national electronic bulletin board service that provides an overview of SBA information.

1-800-859-INFO if you use a 2400 baud modem or 800-697-INFO if you use a 9600 baud modem

See also following entry.

Service Corps of Retired Executives (SCORE)
PO Box 15434
Fort Worth, TX 76119

Retired business executives offer their expertise and services to entrepreneurs through SBA's SCORE, which charges for out-of-pocket expenses but not for the consultant's time.

Telephone Company

Consult your local phone company. Most offer a variety of services and publications for small businesses.

AT&T 800-Number Information
Call 1-800-272-0400.

Trade Associations

National Association of Temporary Services

119 South Saint Asaph Street
Alexandria, VA 22314
(703)549-6287

Books

General Reference Books & Periodicals

Note: Many of the following resources are available through the Research Desk at your local library.

A Consumer's Guide to Telephone Service
Consumer Information Center, Pueblo, CO 81009

Bacon's Publicity Checker
A comprehensive listing of every major newspaper in the United States and Canada.

Directory of Publications and Broadcast Media
Published annually by Gale Research Company, Detroit, MI.

The Dun & Bradstreet Middle Market Directory and *The Dun & Bradstreet Million Dollar Directory*
The Dun & Bradstreet Corporation, New York, NY

Encyclopedia of Associations
Published annually by Gale Research Company, Detroit, MI.

Encyclopedia of Business Information Sources
Published periodically by Gale Research Company, Detroit, MI.

Poor's Register of Corporations, Directors, and Executives
New York, NY: Standard & Poor's Corporation

Tax Guide for Small Businesses
Internal Revenue Service publication. Published annually. Available from local IRS office.

Thomas Register of American Manufacturers
Thomas Publishing Company, New York, NY

Ulrich's International Periodicals Directory
Comprehensive listing of major magazines and newspapers.

Where to Find Business Information
by David Brownstone and Gorton Carruth
New York: John Wiley & Sons, 1982

Magazines

General Business

Business Marketing
Crain Communications, Inc.
740 N. Rush Street
Chicago, IL 60611

Published monthly.

Entrepreneur Magazine
2392 Morse Avenue
Irvine, CA 92714
Published monthly.

Sales & Marketing Management
Bill Communications, Inc.
355 Park Avenue South
New York, NY 10010

Published monthly except in June, August, and October, when it is published twice a month.

Trade

HR Magazine and HR News
606 N. Washington Street
Alexandria, VA 22314
(703)548-3440

Personnel Journal
245 Fischer Avenue, B2
Costa Mesa, CA 92626
(714)751-1883

The Personnel News
4701 Patrick Henry Drive, #1301
Santa Clara, CA 95054
(408)988-8991

INDEX

A

Accounting services, 95, 97, 102
Adding machine, 70
Advertising, 35, 42, 44, 179–190
 appearance, 180–181
 classified, 183–184
 cost of, 188
 designing, 185–186
 display, 184–187, 190
 effectiveness of, 187, 188–189, 198
 ongoing, 180
 specialty, 182, 193, 194–195
 start-up, 180
 tracking response to, 187
Answering machines, 70–71
Apple Macintosh, 79–80
Attorneys, 95, 96–97
Auctions, buying computer equipment at, 89–90

B

Background, of temporary help agency owners, 27
Balance sheet, 122, 130, 141, 142, 147–148
Balloon payment, on leased equipment, 91
Bank account, opening, 110
Bank statement reconciliation, 141, 148–149
Bankruptcy, 4

Banks, obtaining loans from, 127–128, 129–130
Billing, of clients, 169
Bookcases, 71
Bookkeeping systems, 140, 141–148
Borrowing. *See* Financing
Break-even point, 153–154
Brochures, 193
Business Capabilities Application (BCA), 19–22
Business cards, 114
Business failure, 3, 4, 125
Business groups, 195
Business license, 103
Business meetings, 166
Business plan, 117–123
Business records. *See* Record keeping
Businesses
 home-based, 55–63
 legal forms of, 104–106
 naming of, 109–114
 new, 1
 part-time, 126
 See also Small businesses

C

Call forwarding, 61
Call waiting, 61
Capital, 125
Cash flow, 140
Cash Flow Statement, 67, 68–69, 76, 125
Cash journal, 141, 142, 145, 146